365 Fascinating Facts ABOUT

JESUS

Author: Wallis Metts

☙ 1 ❧

A King Will Come

Genesis 49:10 says that a king will come from Judah and that all the nations will obey him. Jesus, of course, was from this tribe, and Bible scholars say this is only one of many promises about him. As many as 250 references are made to Jesus in the books of the Old Testament, written before he was born.

☙ 2 ❧

Jesus and His Cousin

In 4 B.C., two babies were born, cousins named John and Jesus. The lives of these cousins shared several similarities. Both sets of parents were visited by angels and were told that their child would do great things. Both men would die violently in their early 30s. And the world would never be the same.

☙ 3 ❧

When Was Jesus Born?

A sixth-century scholar named Dionysius developed the Christian calendar, which we still use. He calculated that Jesus was born in the 28th year of Augustus, the Roman emperor. Most scholars now agree that the good monk got it wrong, and that Jesus was most likely born four or five years earlier, in 4 B.C.

∞ 4 ∞

When Jesus Wept

The shortest verse in the Bible tells us "Jesus wept" (John 11:35). He also wept over Jerusalem as he considered the fate of the city that had rejected the prophets (see Luke 19:41). His weeping was not uncommon: "During the days of Jesus' life on earth, he offered up prayers and petitions with fervent cries and tears to the one who could save him from death" (Hebrews 5:7, NIV).

∞ 5 ∞

Jesus Knew the Plan

When Jesus told his disciples he would die and then rise again, Peter took him aside and told him he shouldn't talk like that. But Jesus rebuked his disciple: "Get behind Me, Satan! For you are not mindful of the things of God, but the things of men" (Mark 8:33). Christ's death was clearly part of the plan.

∞ 6 ∞

The Gentle Lion

In Revelation, Jesus is called the Lion of the tribe of Judah (5:1–5). In C. S. Lewis' *Chronicles of Narnia,* Christ is represented by a lion named Aslan, the "son of the King from across the sea." Many have been comforted by this depiction, for Aslan is not only bold, courageous, and strong, but also gentle, kind, and sacrificial—like Jesus.

∽ 7 ∾

Modern-Day Christ Figure

In Joseph Girzone's novel *Joshua,* the title character is a young carpenter who comes to a small town and acquires a following. Children see him do "magical" tricks, people are healed, and eventually the pope summons him for a review of his beliefs. After convincing the pope he is real, Joshua disappears, leaving behind a legacy of love and hope, as well as angry religious leaders whose authority has been challenged.

∽ 8 ∾

Jesus Went to Harvard (Sort Of)

Many universities were originally based on dedication to the "principles of Christ." In 1646, Harvard University's "Rules and Precepts" included: "Every one shall consider the main end of his life and study to know God and Jesus Christ which is eternal life." Fifty-two percent of 17th-century Harvard graduates became ministers.

∽ 9 ∾

Jesus Turns Water into Lots of Wine

Early in his ministry, Jesus was at a wedding in Cana when the wine ran out. His mother Mary asked for his help. The celebration would last at least a week, so Jesus had the servants fill six stone pots—about 30 gallons each—with fresh water; he then turned it into wine. *Lots* of wine. This was his first miracle (John 2:11).

∽ **10** ∽

Zacharias Was Speechless

When an elderly priest named Zacharias was chosen to burn incense in the temple, an angel appeared to tell him that he and his wife would have a son. The son, Jesus' cousin, would be John the Baptist. He would "make ready a people prepared for the Lord" (Luke 1:17). Zacharias would not believe it, and the angel took his voice away. He didn't speak again until John was born.

∽ **11** ∽

What's in a Name?

Jesus' last name wasn't "Christ." Normally he would have gone by Joshua ben Joseph, and he was probably known that way in Nazareth. Jesus' ancestry can be traced back to King David on both sides of his family, through Joseph in Matthew's Gospel and through Mary in Luke's.

∽ **12** ∽

Jesus Talks about Money

Jesus talked a lot about money. In fact, he talked about it more often than he talked about heaven or hell. He told 38 parables, and 16 of them dealt with how to handle or think about our possessions and our wealth. While there are about 500 verses in the Bible about prayer, there are over 2,000 about money—most are cautionary.

⌒ **13** ⌒

A Preview of Christ's Pain

Psalm 22 gives an amazing image of someone dying on a cross—written at least 500 years before the Persians invented crucifixion, and 900 years before Christ. Several details match the New Testament accounts of Christ's Crucifixion, including what Jesus would say, what his mockers would say, and that soldiers would gamble for his robe.

⌒ **14** ⌒

Genealogy in Matthew

Only four women are mentioned in Matthew's list of Jesus' ancestors: Tamar pretended to be a prostitute, Rahab was a prostitute, Bathsheba was an adulteress, and Mary, his mother, was probably considered an unwed mother. God often uses and blesses those whom others look down upon.

⌒ **15** ⌒

Josephus on Jesus

A Jewish historian named Josephus, writing about A.D. 94, refers to Jesus twice and John the Baptist once. Even though Josephus was not a Christian, he says Jesus was a "wise man" who did "wonderful works" and says that "those that loved him at the first did not forsake him" after he was crucified.

∞ 16 ∞

Jesus in the History Books

One of the first nonbiblical references to Jesus and his death was by Tacitus, around A.D. 112. Referring to the Roman emperor Nero, who had blamed Christians for the burning of Rome in A.D. 64, Tacitus wrote: "Christus, the founder of the name, was put to death by Pontius Pilate."

∞ 17 ∞

A Satirist's Take

A Greek satirist from the second century, Lucian of Samosata, wrote that Christians "worship a man to this day.... who introduced their novel rites, and was crucified on that account." He found it laughable that Jesus taught them "they are all brothers, from the moment that they are converted."

∞ 18 ∞

Jesus Was Multilingual

Most everyday conversation in Palestine was in Aramaic, but Jesus also knew Hebrew, which was used in the synagogues and the temple, as well as in many Jewish homes. The trade language of the day was Greek, spoken to foreigners (including the Romans) since the time of Alexander the Great.

⌒ 19 ⌒

The Big Picture

The four Gospels give us an account of Christ's life. Matthew, Mark, and Luke are more chronological, yet they start at different points and include different details. John's Gospel is an essay that makes certain points to prove that Jesus was the Son of God. A book or chart that puts these events in order is called a Harmony of the Gospel.

⌒ 20 ⌒

A City for Kings

Micah predicted that Jesus would be born in Bethlehem about 700 years before it happened. So when the magi came to Jerusalem seeking an infant king, officials there could point them to Bethlehem, where King David had also been born. Mathew, Luke, and John all quote Micah. (See Micah 5:2.)

⌒ 21 ⌒

The First 30 Years

The Bible tells us about the birth of Jesus, and about a trip his family took to the temple when he was 12 years old. Other than that, we know little about his life until he began his ministry at the age of 30. We assume he was a carpenter because he was a carpenter's son. (See Mark 6:3 and Matthew 13:55.)

✂ 22 ✂

Did Jesus Have a Beard?

There is no reference to the word "beard" in the entire New Testament, and the earliest depictions of Jesus show him as clean-shaven. On the other hand, Old Testament law required Jewish men to "not cut the hair at the sides of your head." One reference in Isaiah refers to hair being plucked from his cheek, although there is no word on its length.

✂ 23 ✂

"How Can This Be?"

Mary asked this question when the angel told her she would have a son. She did "not know a man," as she put it (Luke 1:34). But the angel said, "The Holy Spirit will come upon you," and Mary replied, "Let it be to me according to your word" (1:35, 38). The Virgin Birth is mentioned by both Luke and Matthew, and has been a central belief since the earliest days of the Church.

✂ 24 ✂

Herod the Not-So-Great

Herod the Great ruled Israel in the time of Christ. He was a vicious man, who killed several of his ten wives and two of his sons. He is said to have had people executed almost daily. Herod was the one who ordered his soldiers to kill all of the infant boys in Bethlehem to keep Jesus from becoming king.

❧ 25 ❧

When Was Jesus Born?

Jesus was probably not born on December 25th. While the weather in Bethlehem was fairly mild, shepherds were not likely to be out in the fields at night during the winter. The December date was not set until after A.D. 300, and may have been a way to offset the pagan celebration of the Winter Solstice.

❧ 26 ❧

A Taxing Situation

When a Roman emperor required everyone to be registered for tax purposes, he had no idea that this would move Mary and Joseph from their home in Nazareth to Bethlehem—just in time for Jesus to be born in their ancient tribal home. Proverbs 21:1 says, "The king's heart is in the hand of the Lord."

❧ 27 ❧

A Son of the Commandment

When Jesus was 12 years old, his family took him to the temple. At that age a young man became a "son of the commandment," personally responsible for knowing and keeping the Law. Even after his parents had started home, Jesus remained, listening to the elders teach and asking them questions. This, he said, was "My Father's business" (Luke 2:49).

∽ **28** ∽

Face to Face

Only one Bible writer describes Jesus' appearance, and this is only after Jesus returns to heaven. In Revelation, the last book in the Bible, the Apostle John says, "His head and hair were white like wool...and His eyes like a flame of fire; His feet were like fine brass, as if refined in a furnace, and His voice as the sound of many waters" (1:14–15).

∽ **29** ∽

Star Seekers

The magi who came looking for Jesus probably came a year or more after Jesus was born. They were following a star, one which they likely believed was prophesied about 1,400 years earlier by Balaam: "A Star shall come out of Jacob; A Scepter shall rise out of Israel" (Numbers 24:17).

∽ **30** ∽

Did Jesus Laugh?

We are never told that Jesus laughed, but children were attracted to him, and he was often welcome at parties with tax collectors and prostitutes. This suggests a welcoming demeanor toward those who are often overlooked or mistreated. And his Father laughs—see Psalm 59:8—so it's likely he did, too!

∞ **31** ∞

Say What?

Jesus may be the most frequently quoted individual in history, but John Bartlett's famous 1919 collection of over 11,000 quotes doesn't quote him at all.

∞ **32** ∞

A Fishy Story

The annual temple tax on Jewish men was a half shekel, equal to about two days' pay. When Peter spoke to Jesus about paying taxes, Jesus sent him out to catch a fish (Matthew 17:24–27). Jesus said the fish would have a large shekel coin in its mouth—enough to pay the annual tax for both of them.

∞ **33** ∞

Food for Thought

After his resurrection, Jesus appeared to his disciples several times. Once he even fixed breakfast for them: Fish were roasting over a fire as they came in from their boats after fishing all night (John 21:9). On another occasion he ate with them, proving he was not a ghost (Luke 24:41–43).

∽ 34 ∽

Where Was Everybody?

Only one of the 12 disciples was at the cross when Jesus died. All the rest had fled, but John—the youngest of the disciples—was there. From the cross, Jesus asked him to take care of his mother, Mary, who was also there with some of her friends.

∽ 35 ∽

He Wasn't Weak

After he was baptized by John the Baptist, Jesus went into an extremely rugged wilderness near the Jordan River. There, after going without food for 40 days, he was tempted by Satan. Throughout the Gospels Jesus is often walking great distances or staying up all night to pray.

∽ 36 ∽

In the Beginning Was the Word

The first few sentences of the Gospel of John were from a song that the early church sang about the deity of Christ. The Apostle John spent three years with Jesus, but by the time he wrote his gospel, he had had 50 years to reflect on his experience. His account is different from the other three Gospels, but not contradictory.

∽ **37** ∾

The Glory Revealed

In the first chapter of his Gospel, the Apostle John argues that the Word has a name—Jesus. The Word, he says, "became flesh and dwelt among us, and we beheld His glory" (John 1:14). The Greeks, the Romans, the Egyptians, the Assyrians, the Jews—everyone at that time used the idea of the Word to describe God's character or personality.

∽ **38** ∾

Jesus Raised the Dead

Jesus raised not one, not two, but three people from the dead. He raised the son of a widow from Nain when he encountered his funeral procession. Then he raised the 12-year-old daughter of Jairus, the leader of a synagogue. And finally he raised his friend Lazarus, the brother of Mary and Martha.

∽ **39** ∾

At the Funeral Procession

Today, when a funeral procession passes, we pull off the road and wait—but according to Jewish tradition, you join it. This was the situation when Jesus raised the adult son of the widow from Nain from the dead. "He had compassion on her," Luke writes (Luke 7:13). She had lost her husband and her only son, and there was no one to take care of her.

∞ **40** ∞

The First Promise

After Eve ate the forbidden fruit in the Garden of Eden, God told the serpent Satan that there would be "enmity" between serpents and women, and that her offspring "will crush your head" (Genesis 3:15, NIV). This is the first promise of Jesus in the Bible.

∞ **41** ∞

The Pool at Bethesda

People believed that an angel stirred the water at the Pool of Bethesda, and that whenever this occurred, the first person in the pool would be healed. Jesus healed a lame man there because the man could never get into the water in time. "Stand up, take your mat and walk," Jesus said (John 5:8, NRSV). The man had been lame for almost 40 years.

∞ **42** ∞

Keep It Quiet

Several times when Jesus healed someone, he told that person not to tell anyone about it. For example, he gave this command to a couple of blind men after healing them, but they told others anyway (Matthew 9:27–31). Scholars say that either Jesus did not want the miracles to distract from what he was trying to teach, or he wanted to wait for the right moment to reveal who he was.

❦ 43 ❦

The Gentiles

When one gentile woman asked Jesus to heal her daughter, he said, "It is not good to take the children's bread and throw it to the little dogs" (Matthew 15:26). Jews normally had nothing to do with gentiles and often referred to them this way. Some say Jesus was teasing this woman, and others that he was mocking his disciples who often felt this way. Jesus healed her daughter and then went on to heal many gentiles in the Decapolis east of Galilee.

❦ 44 ❦

The Great Physician

Jesus healed a crippled woman on the Sabbath, and the Jewish leaders were enraged. Even though she had been unable to stand up straight for 18 years, the leader of the synagogue told her she should have come back on a different day to be healed (Luke 13:10–17).

~ 45 ~

Is That Clear?

Sometimes Jesus told parables to make things clear. And sometimes he told parables to make things obscure. Later, he would explain these more obscure parables to his disciples. Some of the things he taught were only for those who were seeking him and believed him (Matthew 13:1–36).

~ 46 ~

What's for Lunch?

Matthew wrote that Jesus fed a crowd of 5,000 with bread and fish, and another time he says Jesus fed a crowd of 4,000 with bread and fish. Which was it? Both are true, actually. Each was a separate incident. Not only are the numbers different, but so are the places, as well as the amount of food they started with and collected afterward (Matthew 14:14–21 and 15:32–39).

~ 47 ~

Please Forgive Me—Again

The rabbis taught that you should forgive someone three times before you could retaliate. Peter asked Jesus how many times you had to forgive someone, thinking seven would be enough. Jesus said not seven times, but seventy times seven, or 490 times (Matthew 18:21–22).

✑ **48** ✑

A Passover Premonition

At Passover, ancient Jews slaughtered a lamb and then splashed its blood on the lintels of the door, at the top and on the sides. Christians believe this pictures a person splayed out on a cross. John the Baptist called Jesus the "Lamb of God" (John 1:29).

✑ **49** ✑

Size Doesn't Matter

When a widow dropped two "mites" into the treasury at the temple, Jesus said she had actually given more than all the rich men who paraded their wealth and dumped in fortunes. "Out of her poverty [she] put in all that she had," he said (Mark 12:44). A mite was a small coin, worth less than a penny.

✑ **50** ✑

One of Many Miracles

The Bible records several instances in which God grants someone a child under miraculous circumstances: Sarah had Isaac at 90. Although they were barren, he gave Samuel to Hannah, Jacob and Esau to Rebekah, Joseph to Rachel, and John the Baptist to Elizabeth. Mary, a virgin, was the mother of Jesus.

⣫ **51** ⣫

Not a Hometown Hero

One Sabbath at the synagogue in his hometown of Nazareth, Jesus read from the scriptures about the Messiah coming. Then he said the passage referred to him, but that he was not going to heal anyone there. The people of Nazareth were so angry that they tried to throw him off a cliff. (See Luke 4:16–30.)

⣫ **52** ⣫

Six Sermons in the Gospels

Jesus gave six lengthy discourses in scripture, plus many other teachings. Any of them can be read in a short amount of time. The most famous of these is the Sermon on the Mount (see Matthew 5). Each Gospel writer tended to share different points from what was probably a longer speech, so seeing the big picture usually requires comparing the different accounts.

⣫ **53** ⣫

More Than Twelve

We tend to think of only twelve disciples, but Jesus had more followers than that. At one time he sent out 70 others to preach (Luke 10:1). After the resurrection he appeared to at least 500 of them at one time (see 1 Corinthians 15:6). The Twelve were especially close to him, and were later called apostles.

↷ **54** ↶

No Miracles on Demand

At Jesus' trial, when Pontius Pilate heard Jesus was from Galilee, he sent him to King Herod, who was visiting Jerusalem at that time. Herod had heard of Jesus and wanted him to do a miracle, but Jesus refused. In fact, he wouldn't even speak to him. (See Luke 23:6–12.)

↷ **55** ↶

Who Is This Man?

The Bible recounts 12 different occasions when Jesus appeared to his followers after his resurrection, but they didn't always realize it was him at first. Mary Magdalene thought he was a gardener and didn't recognize him until he called her name (John 20:14–16). Two disciples on the Road to Emmaus didn't know him until he prayed (Luke 24:13-35).

↷ **56** ↶

Born Again

Jesus was the first one to use the term "born again," in conversation with a Jewish leader named Nicodemus. Nicodemus was confused by this, but Jesus explained that he was talking about a spiritual birth, not a physical one. Without this, Jesus said, one "cannot see the kingdom of God" (John 3:3).

ᕲ **57** ᕲ

Price of a Slave

In Exodus 21, the value of a slave was 30 silver shekels—about three months' wages. This is the amount Judas was paid to betray Jesus. According to the Gospel of Matthew, Judas returned the money (before hanging himself), and the elders used it to buy a potter's field—a small plot filled with broken pottery and other trash that would be used to bury poor people (27:3–10).

ᕲ **58** ᕲ

How Long Was Jesus on the Cross?

Jesus was on the cross about six or seven hours, from midmorning to late afternoon. Sometimes it could take three or four days to die on a cross, but Jesus had been tried and tortured for hours before his Crucifixion. But John says he died when he was ready: "bowing His head, He gave up His spirit" (John 19:30).

ᕲ **59** ᕲ

A Seamless Garment

Although he was poor, Jesus had an expensive tunic—one with no seams, woven out of a single piece of cloth. It was probably a gift. The soldiers who crucified him decided not to tear it, but to cast dice for it (John 19:24).

❧ 60 ❧
Birthday Rites

Three traditional ceremonies were observed when Jesus was born. On the eighth day he was named and circumcised. About six weeks later, his parents traveled to Jerusalem and paid five shekels to "redeem the firstborn," essentially to buy him back since the firstborn belonged to God. At this time his mother also offered a sacrifice as part of a purification ritual. She offered two doves or pigeons because they could not afford a lamb.

❧ 61 ❧
Da Vinci Got It Wrong

Leonardo da Vinci's famous painting *The Last Supper* shows Jesus and his disciples sitting at a table. The custom, however, was to recline on your elbows around a mat or a very low table.

❧ 62 ❧
Left Out Something Important

Thomas Jefferson didn't believe in miracles, including the resurrection. He printed his own special edition of the Bible with no references to the supernatural, concentrating only on Jesus' moral teachings. The last words of this Bible were: "There laid they Jesus, And rolled a great stone to the door of the sepulchre, and departed."

☙ **63** ❧

Learned Something Important

A Civil War general named Lew Wallace set out to write a book to prove that Jesus was not divine. He was converted in the process and instead wrote *Ben-Hur: A Tale of the Christ,* a best-selling novel that was later turned into the Oscar-winning movie starring Charlton Heston. Considered one of the most influential Christian books of the 19th century, it has never been out of print and has been adapted for film four times.

☙ **64** ❧

The Point of the Story

The front of St. Paul's Cathedral in London is a 70-foot carved screen, primarily of marble and brass. Various scenes are portrayed, with a large sculpture of the suffering Christ as the centerpiece. The inscription underneath says, "Sic Deus dilexit mundum." The Latin phrase means: "So God loved the world!"

☙ **65** ❧

John the Baptist

In various churches all over Europe are three shoulder blades, four legs, and five arms that are supposed to have belonged to John the Baptist. There are also 50 index fingers, all relics that John the Baptist is reported to have used when he pointed to Jesus and called him the "Lamb of God."

☙ **66** ❧

Teenage Jesus

Some of the apocryphal gospel accounts, written in the second and third centuries, purport to tell us about Jesus as a young man. They claim Jesus made clay sparrows, threw them into the air, and turned them into real birds. And when his playmates irritated him, he turned them into goats.

☙ **67** ❧

Happy Caravansary!

A caravansary was a compound built around a water supply that housed traveling merchants, soldiers, pilgrims, and others. The "inn" where Mary and Joseph stayed was probably a caravansary, where camel drivers and muleteers would have gathered to swap stories, drink, and tell jokes.

∞ **68** ∞

A Great City

Judaism, Christianity, and Islam all regard Jerusalem as a holy city. Jesus told his disciples that the city would be flattened, that "not one stone shall be left upon another" (Mark 13:2). According to the first-century Jewish historian Josephus, this happened in A.D. 70, when the Roman general Titus—who would later become emperor—broke down the wall and killed more than a million people.

∞ **69** ∞

At Least One Revolutionary

One of Jesus' disciples, Simon the Zealot, was a terrorist—at least to the Romans. The Zealots were bent on driving the Romans out of Palestine. Simon is only mentioned three times. Since Jesus also selected Matthew—who was a tax collector for the Romans—as a disciple, he was clearly reaching out to everyone.

∞ **70** ∞

Who Caesar Is Not

Polycarp (A.D. 70–155), one of the early church fathers, was put to death by the Romans. When offered the opportunity to say "Caesar is Lord" and be spared, he replied: "For eighty-six years I have been the servant of Jesus Christ and he never did me any injury. How then can I blaspheme my King who saved me?"

⁓ **71** ⁓

Obey Your Father

The book of Hebrews says that Jesus "learned obedience by the things which He suffered" (5:8). Some consider Jesus the ultimate "free" man, but repeatedly he is said to be "in submission" to the Father. In Gethsemane, he asked his Father to "let this cup pass from Me" (Matthew 26:39), but the Father decreed that he should die for our sins, and he went to the cross willingly.

⁓ **72** ⁓

The Town Dump

When Jesus spoke of "hell" in the scriptures, he usually used the word "gehenna." This was the town dump outside of Jerusalem, where fires burned day and night and worms lived in the refuse. Thus Jesus used the expression, speaking of hell, "Their worm does not die, and the fire is not quenched" (Mark 9:48).

⁓ **73** ⁓

What's in a Name?

According to Billy Graham, there are 265 names for Christ in the Bible. Among them: Jesus, Lord, Savior, Friend, Good Shepherd, Life, Way, Truth, Resurrection, Light, Bread of Life, King of Kings, Lord of Lords, Master, Son of God, Son of Man, Wonderful Counselor, Mighty God, Everlasting Father, and Prince of Peace.

∽ 74 ∽

A Cruel Beating

When Roman soldiers flogged a prisoner in preparation for crucifixion, the victim was tied to a pole or beam so he would not fall down—even if he lost consciousness. They used a whip with leather strands, tied at points into knots that held pieces of metal and bone. The idea was to lash with the whip and then rip it sideways, tearing the flesh of the victim as much as possible.

∽ 75 ∽

A True Servant

Washing the feet of guests was common in the dry, dusty climate of Palestine, although it was usually done by slaves or servants, or sometimes women or children. Abraham offered this gesture to an angel, as did Abigail to King David, and a prostitute to Jesus. Then Jesus offered it himself, for his disciples, before the Last Supper.

∽ 76 ∽

The Name of Jesus

The name Jesus originated from the Latin form of the Greek Iesous, a form of the Hebrew Yeshua. It can also be translated as Joshua or Yesua. Yesua means "Yahweh (God) delivers, or rescues." An angel told Joseph to name Mary's son Jesus, "for He will save His people from their sins" (Matthew 1:21).

∞ **77** ∞

Could Jesus Read?

Although in Jesus' day only a few people could read—and fewer still could write—it is clear Jesus could do both. We see him reading in the synagogue and writing in the dirt. The synagogue was the central institution for Jews outside the temple, and some ability to read Hebrew was expected of most men.

∞ **78** ∞

Did Jesus Have Any Siblings?

Jesus had several people who were called brothers and sisters; they may have been half brothers and sisters, stepsiblings, or possibly cousins (Matthew 12:46–47; 13:55–56). His brothers included James, Joses, Simon, and Judas. His sisters are not named in the Bible. Although they have similar names, none of his brothers were apostles, but James did become the head of the church in Jerusalem.

∞ **79** ∞

Simon and His Sons

Simon of Cyrene was conscripted to help Jesus carry the cross up to Golgotha. Simon had two sons who were apparently known to the early church. Mark 15:21 says Simon was the father of Alexander and Rufus, as if the readers of the Gospel would know those two men.

∽ **80** ∾

What Jesus Ate

Jesus ate bread (Matthew 26:26), a staple throughout history. He ate clean meats such as lamb (Luke 22:15) and fish (Matthew 14:19). He may have eaten eggs, which he lists among several "good gifts" (Luke 11:12–13). One prophecy says Jesus would eat butter and honey (Isaiah 7:15). After the resurrection we are told Jesus ate broiled fish and honeycomb (Luke 24:42–43).

∽ **81** ∾

Was Jesus a Carpenter?

The word translated from Hebrew as "carpenter" is *tekton,* a generic word for anyone who makes things. The word is applied to craftsmen of all sorts, but more frequently a builder. Early writings and tradition indicate Jesus worked with wood in some form—hence, carpenter.

∽ **82** ∾

The Meaning of Messiah

Jews in Christ's time were waiting for the Messiah, who they hoped would renew David's kingdom and defeat the Romans. The word means "Anointed One," and is also translated as "Christ." In the New Testament the word is used about 500 times to refer to Jesus, who said he came to set up a spiritual kingdom.

⊂∞ **83** ∞⊃

Was Jesus a Real Rabbi?

A rabbi was someone respected for their knowledge and understanding. The word comes from a Hebrew word that means "Great One" and had come to mean "teacher" or "master." Jesus never objected to being called rabbi or master, although he cautioned the elders and his disciples not to seek such titles, because "whoever exalts himself will be humbled" (Matthew 23:12).

∞ **84** ∞

Did Jesus Sing?

Singing is common in the Bible, and the early church was commanded to do it (see Ephesians 5:19). The book of Psalms is in fact a book of hymns, used for thousands of years by Jews. Jesus himself sang at least once. After the Lord's Supper, before Jesus and his disciples traveled to the Garden of Gethsemane, both Matthew and Mark tell us, "and when they had sung a hymn, they went out" (Matthew 26:30; Mark 14:26).

⊂∞ **85** ∞⊃

To See the Glory

George Frideric Handel composed his masterpiece, the *Messiah*, in 23 straight days, often going without food. When he reached the "Hallelujah" chorus, he said, "I did think I did see all Heaven before me, and the great God Himself."

∽ **86** ∽

Why Was Jesus Baptized?

John the Baptist protested when Jesus wanted to be baptized, because he knew Jesus did not have to repent of any sins. But Jesus insisted, because he wanted to identify with his cousin John and the people he was baptizing. He was saying he wanted to live a righteous life under God's rules.

∽ **87** ∽

Jesus as God

The term "Trinity" is never used in the Bible, but the Old Testament refers to God in the plural while also referring to him as one. And the New Testament also refers to the Father, Son, and Spirit as God 17 times. Jesus also claimed to be one with God on several occasions.

∽ **88** ∽

Mad at the Money Changers

Jesus drove the money changers out of the temple because they were overcharging the people. Adult men had to pay a half shekel each year to help maintain the temple—about two days' wages. To do this, foreign money had to be exchanged into official temple money, and the exchange rate was as high as 8:1.

∞ **89** ∞
The Problem of Publicans

The Roman Senate farmed out the collection of taxes to entrepreneurs, usually from the privileged classes. These investors would hire a "magister" to oversee a five-year contract, and they would hire and oversee tax collectors who were encouraged to charge as much as possible. These are referred to as "publicans" in the New Testament, and Jesus made friends with some of them—most notably Matthew, one of his disciples, and Zacchaeus, well-known for fraud.

∞ **90** ∞
Kiss My Hand

The Greek word for worship literally means "to kiss," referring to paying homage to a king by kissing his hand. When Satan tempted Jesus to "worship" him in the wilderness in Matthew 4:9, he was saying, "kiss my hand and recognize me as a legitimate ruler."

∞ **91** ∞
Receiving Him

In John's Gospel, Jesus describes being born again as "receiving" him. The original word is used to describe a man taking a wife or adopting a child, constituting a committed, lifelong relationship with another.

◐ **92** ◑

Take My Coat

An essential part of Hebrew attire was a cloak, an outer garment worn like a sport coat or jacket. It was little more than a square cloth with a hole for one's head. The color and quality varied, however, and it could be used as collateral, provided it was returned to the owner by night so he or she could use it as a blanket. This is the garment people spread along the street when Jesus entered Jerusalem.

◐ **93** ◑

God So Loved the World

John 3:16, one of the most well-known verses in the Bible, was originally much more shocking than we realize today. Jews believed that God loved them, but no one else. They generally looked down upon sinners and gentiles, but Jesus said, *"God so loved the world."* Jews at the time found this very difficult to believe.

❧ **94** ❧

Take the Short Road

Although the route was much longer, devout Jews would go around Samaria on the way between Jerusalem and Galilee. The Samaritans were despised because they were viewed as a mixed race that practiced a corrupt form of Jewish worship at Mount Gerizim rather than at Jerusalem. The woman Jesus encountered at the well in John 4 was a Samaritan. Jesus also told a well-known story about the Good Samaritan.

❧ **95** ❧

What Is a Synagogue?

The synagogue became the center of Jewish community life when the Jews were exiled to Babylon (597 B.C.) and the temple was destroyed. Even though Herod had rebuilt the temple by the time of Jesus, the synagogue still functioned in each town as a school, social center, and meeting place.

❧ **96** ❧

The Bima

Jesus attended synagogue each Sabbath and often preached there. The custom was for seven men to mount the platform called a bima and read from the scriptures. According to custom, the reader would read in Hebrew while an interpreter would translate it into Aramaic, the everyday language. Then the man would sit down and explain what he had read.

∽ 97 ∾

Belonging to Christ

Early believers called themselves "brothers," "saints," or "disciples," but gentiles called them "Christians" so as to differentiate them from Jews. The word is thought to have originated in Antioch, as a combination of the Greek *Christos* and the Latin *ianus,* meaning "that belong to Christ." It is believed the term contained some element of ridicule.

∽ 98 ∾

A Free Man

When Jesus cast out a demon (Luke 4:35–36), the people said he had power and authority. The Greek word translated as "authority" means freedom of choice and action. What they meant was that Jesus acted spontaneously, on his own, without permission.

∽ 99 ∾

Name That Apostle

The apostles were a close-knit group, with two or three sets of brothers and possibly one father and son. There were also two called James, two called Simon, and two called Judas. Some of them were referred to with nicknames—"the Zealot," "the Twin," and the "Sons of Thunder."

∞ **100** ∞

That Smells Nice

Frankincense and myrrh, gifts brought to the baby Jesus by the magi, were both expensive substances used to mask body odor, among other things. Baths and showers were not common, and frankincense was sometimes rubbed directly on the skin as a kind of deodorant. Women would stand over burning myrrh and allow the fragrance to permeate their clothes and hair before going out in public.

∞ **101** ∞

The King of the Jews

The cross is often depicted with the acronym INRI. It stands for "Iesus Nazarenus Rex Iudaerum," Latin for "Jesus the Nazarene, the King of the Jews." The Romans typically crucified people near a highway, so this would have been seen by Jewish people from many countries as they were streaming into Jerusalem for the Passover.

∞ **102** ∞

Happy Birthday to Jesus

Early Christian writers often mocked the idea of celebrating a birthday as pagan. But about 200 years after Jesus lived, Egyptian Christians began to celebrate his birthday on May 20. Other Christian groups also celebrated it during March, April, or January.

∞ 103 ∞

The Star of Bethlehem

The magi were intrigued by some celestial event, the "star" they followed to Bethlehem looking for a newborn king. Some believe this was the alignment of Jupiter (named after the Greek father of the gods) and Venus (named after the goddess of fertility). Such an alignment occurred in August of 3 B.C.

∞ 104 ∞

All In a Day's Work

The coin Jesus referred to when he said to "give back to Caesar what is Caesar's" was probably a denarius (Matthew 22:21, NIV). This small, silver Roman coin was equivalent to a laborer's wage for a day's work. The "widow's mite" he noticed in the temple was likely a lepton, the coin of least value at that time.

∞ 105 ∞

A Small Sea

The Sea of Galilee is the world's lowest freshwater lake, at 680 feet below sea level. It is about 13 miles long and 8 miles wide and is also known as the Lake of Chinnereth, the Sea of Tiberias, and the Lake of Gennesaret. Several of the disciples were fishermen on this lake, home to over 40 species of fish, which were dried or salted and exported throughout the region.

∾ 106 ∾
When Shiloh Comes

The word "Shiloh" was used in Genesis 49:10 as an early reference to the Messiah: "The scepter shall not depart from Judah, Nor a lawgiver from between his feet, Until Shiloh comes." The word means "to rest" or "to give rest." Jesus said to come to him and he would "give you rest" (Matthew 11:28).

∾ 107 ∾
A House of Bread

The name of Bethlehem, where Jesus was born, means "house of bread." Jacob buried his beloved wife Rachel near there, and it was the hometown of King David. It was also the hometown of Ibzan, one of the judges, and Boaz, who married Ruth. It is about five miles south of Jerusalem and overlooked an ancient highway from Hebron to Egypt.

∾ 108 ∾
Down on the Farm

Nazareth, the childhood home of Jesus, was high in a sheltered valley, some 1,300 feet above sea level. The first-century Jewish historian Josephus said the area was so fertile that "even the most indolent...are tempted to devote themselves to agriculture." Jesus is thought to have drawn many of his rural illustrations from his childhood in this farming community.

∞ 109 ∞
Seven Titles

There are seven titles for Jesus in the first chapter of John alone. In this one passage of scripture, he is called the Word of God, the Lamb of God, the Son of God, Rabbi, Messiah, the King of Israel, and the Son of Man.

∞ 110 ∞
Palms and Posterity

The date palm can live for 200 years, and along with other types of palms in the region, it provided wax, sugar, dyes, resin, and an alcoholic drink. It became a symbol of the righteous enjoying well-deserved prosperity, which partly explains the expectation of the crowds who lined the street waving palm leaves as Jesus entered Jerusalem. They wanted Jesus to become king and overthrow the Romans, ushering in a new age of prosperity.

∞ 111 ∞
The Salt of the Earth

Salt was used to seal covenants because its preservative qualities made it a fitting symbol for long-lasting agreements. The Arab expression "there is salt between us" meant an agreement had been reached. When Jesus said his followers should be "the salt of the earth" (Matthew 5:13), he was suggesting something about the quality of our relationships with each other.

❦ **112** ❧

Succinctly Said

Shakespeare wrote that "brevity is the soul of wit," an observation that has often been demonstrated to be true. The Declaration of Independence is only 300 words, for example, and the Ten Commandments is about the same length. Jesus himself was quite succinct, using fewer than 100 words for the Lord's Prayer.

❦ **113** ❧

Defending the Faith

The Pharisees were a political and religious party that began about 200 years before the life of Christ. The name comes from a word that means "separate," and their original concern was defending Jewish tradition from the influence of Greek culture. They became experts in Old Testament law. There were about 6,000 of them when Jesus was alive.

❦ **114** ❧

Amen and Amen!

When Jesus explained being born again to Nicodemus, three times he said "verily" or "most assuredly." The word is literally "amen" in Hebrew. Nicodemus would have understood this as meaning Jesus was absolutely certain, and the idea was binding and necessary.

❧ 115 ❧
Wash Your Hands

The Pharisees were indignant that Jesus and his disciples did not wash their hands (Mark 7:1–5), but this referred to an elaborate ritual that had little to do with cleanliness. Water was poured over the hands, and had to run from the fingers to the wrist. Everything was regulated, including the shape and size of the container for the water.

❧ 116 ❧
Mary, Mary, Mary, and Mary

At least four women named Mary are noted in connection with the ministry of Jesus. One, of course, was his mother. There was also Mary Magdalene, from whom Jesus cast out demons. She was apparently a woman of some means, who helped fund his ministry. There was also Mary of Bethany, who, with her sister Martha, often provided a place for Jesus to stay. A fourth Mary was the mother of James and John, two of his disciples.

❧ 117 ❧
A City on a Hill

When Jesus referred to a "city on a hill" in the Sermon on the Mount, he may have been thinking of his own hometown of Nazareth. Nazareth was on a hill and its light could be seen from Cana, nine miles away.

⮞ **118** ⮜

Herod's Temple

The temple Jesus went to in Jerusalem was a renovation of the temple that the Jews built after the second exile. To enlarge the temple, King Herod had workers extend a platform over the south end of the temple hill. Part of the retaining wall for this is what we now refer to as the Wailing Wall. Only two stone blocks of the temple itself are known to remain.

⮞ **119** ⮜

That's a Lot of Angels

Emperor Augustus reorganized the Roman army into legions of 6,000 men. These were broken down into "centuries" of 100 men, which were grouped into "cohorts" of 600 men. It is thought that during the life of Christ there were probably only a few cohorts stationed in Israel. When Jesus was arrested, he said his Father could put more than 12 legions of angels at his disposal (Matthew 26:53).

⮞ **120** ⮜

The Living Dead

Suspected lepers were quarantined for seven days and then examined by a priest. If the condition persisted, they were quarantined for another seven days and examined again. At this point, they were forbidden to have any contact with healthy humans, including their own families, and became outcasts and beggars. Jesus healed and befriended many of them.

❧ 121 ❧

Pentecost

The Jewish festival of Pentecost takes its name from a Greek word that means "fifty." It was celebrated fifty days after the consecration of the barley harvest on the second day of Passover. It was also called the Feast of Weeks. It took on special significance for the early church when 120 disciples were filled with the Holy Spirit on Pentecost following Christ's resurrection.

❧ 122 ❧

A Small Seed

The mustard seed referred to in the Gospels was thought at the time to be the smallest of all seeds, though the annual plant grew up to five feet tall. It was cultivated for its oil and also ground into a paste for eating or medicinal purposes.

❧ 123 ❧

A Matter of Emphasis

The name Jesus appears 700 times in the Gospels, which tell the story of his life. However, it appears less than 70 times in the epistles. On the other hand, the name Christ appears about 60 times in the Gospels and the book of Acts, while it occurs 240 times in the epistles and the book of Revelation.

❧ 124 ❧

What Is a Winnowing Fork?

Winnowing involved separating the wheat from its husk and other chaff by beating the grain in some way and then tossing the mixture into the air. The heavier grain would fall to the ground, while the wind would blow the rest away. John the Baptist used this process to describe how Christ would separate believers from unbelievers (Matthew 3:12).

❧ 125 ❧

Many Miracles

In his Gospel, the Apostle John included seven miracles of Jesus from the 37 recorded in the New Testament. There were probably more, as John writes: "And truly Jesus did many other signs in the presence of His disciples, which are not written in this book" (John 20:30).

❧ 126 ❧

Little Fish

The fish became an early and important symbol of Christianity. Abercius, a second-century bishop, writes that churches often ate bread and fish at communion, a reference to Jesus feeding the 5,000. Newly-baptized Christians were also referred to as "little fish." And the Greek word for fish, *Ichthus*, forms an acrostic for "Jesus Christ, Son of God, Savior."

➥ **127** ➥

The Second Calling

John the Baptist introduced some of his disciples to Jesus, and they spent several days with him. Apparently they returned home and Jesus went back later and called them again as apostles. These men included two sets of brothers: Simon Peter and Andrew, as well as James and John. (See Matthew 4:18–22.)

➥ **128** ➥

Pass the Bread

No Jewish meal was complete without bread. Before the meal, the father would break the bread and give thanks, passing it around before the other food was served. A separate blessing was offered for the rest of the meal. This is what was going on at the Last Supper when Jesus first gave thanks, broke the bread, and passed it to his disciples, telling them to "do this in remembrance of Me" (Luke 22:19).

⊙ 129 ⊙

Jewish Converts

Gentiles were converted to Judaism, but often with less than ideal results. Generally, Jews at that time were suspicious of the converts, called proselytes, and considered them genetically blemished and unfit for any leadership role. Jesus was referring to these proselytes when he told the Pharisees that they "bind heavy burdens, hard to bear, and lay them on men's shoulders" (Matthew 23:4).

⊙ 130 ⊙

Seeking to Save

The Pharisees believed that when the Messiah came he would judge gentiles and other sinners, but from the beginning Jesus was more concerned about money changers in the temple and other disturbing aspects of religious tradition. He told Nicodemus, who was a Pharisee, that he did not come to punish sinners but to rescue them. (See John 3.)

⊙ 131 ⊙

The Woman at the Well

The disciples were surprised to find Jesus talking to the woman at the well, not just because she was a woman but also because she was a Samaritan. (See John 4.) The Samaritans did not recognize any prophets after Moses and only accepted the first five books of the Old Testament.

∞ 132 ∞

Everyone Is Welcome

Elijah once found refuge in the home of a pagan widow, and Elisha healed a pagan general named Naaman of leprosy. Jesus pointed to these two examples when he told people from his hometown of Nazareth that "no prophet is accepted in his own country" (Luke 4:24). Over and over again, he asserted that the gospel message was not just for the Jews.

∞ 133 ∞

Mistaken Identity

King Herod believed that Jesus was John the Baptist raised from the dead. Herod, of course, had executed John at the insistence of his wife and her daughter. He was not alone in misreading the teachings and miracles of Jesus in this way. (See Mark 6:14–16.)

∞ 134 ∞

A Lost Coin

Many Jewish women strung together coins from their dowry and wore them around their neck. When Jesus told the parable of the woman who lost a coin, the coin may have been such an heirloom, with as much sentimental value as monetary value. This explains her panic and determination to find the coin. (See Luke 15:8–10).

∞ 135 ∞

An Uncommon Cure

Old Testament law taught that a woman was ceremonially unclean during menstruation. The woman who touched Jesus' robe, believing it would heal her "issue of blood" (Luke 8:43, KJV), had not been able to participate in worship or community life for over 12 years. The Jewish Talmud described 11 different cures for her condition, but none had worked.

∞ 136 ∞

Take Up Your Cross

When Jesus was about ten years old, the Romans crushed a rebellion led by Judas of Galilee and crucified about 2,000 Galileans, leaving their bodies on crosses along the road. When Jesus told his disciples to "take up [their] cross, and follow Me," they had a fresh and vivid memory of what this meant (Matthew 16:24).

∞ 137 ∞

Phony Phylacteries

A phylactery was a small box containing Bible verses, strapped to the wrist or the forehead during prayer. Jesus condemned the practice of drawing attention to oneself in this way (Matthew 23:2–7).

⮑ 138 ⮐

Drinking Blood?

O ld Testament law clearly taught that drinking or eating blood was absolutely forbidden. Even though he was speaking figuratively, Jesus' listeners would have been shocked and repulsed when he said, "Whoever eats My flesh and drinks My blood has eternal life" (John 6:54).

⮑ 139 ⮐

Party Time

T here were essentially three political parties at the time of Christ. The Pharisees were very strict about the Law and were anti-Roman. The Sadducees were more liberal, and hoped to accommodate Rome in some ways. Finally, the Herodians had little theological interest and collaborated with King Herod. All three groups were ultimately allied in putting Jesus to death.

⮑ 140 ⮐

Pay Attention

A lamp was a cotton wick floating in a dish of oil, requiring constant attention to keep it lit. Jesus used this example to suggest his followers should be alert and ready when he returned (Luke 12:35).

∞ **141** ∞

A Perfect Plan

When Jesus told his disciples that he "must" die, he used a word that means something is legally or morally binding. *Dei* is used more than 100 times in the New Testament to refer to or indicate necessity imposed by the will of God. Jesus' trip to the cross was deliberate and calculated. (See Matthew 16:21.)

∞ **142** ∞

Living Water

Each day during the Feast of Tabernacles, a priest would go to the Pool of Siloam and bring a pitcher of water back to the temple and pour it into the base of the altar. As he did this, the crowd would wave palm branches and chant the Hallel (Psalms 113—118). It was on such a day that Jesus stood and cried out, "If anyone thirsts, let him come to Me and drink" (John 7:37).

∞ **143** ∞

The Pursuit of Sinners

The idea that God would pursue sinners to draw them back to him was revolutionary to first-century Jews. While they believed God would receive repentant sinners, they would have found the parable about a shepherd leaving 99 sheep to find a single lost sheep mystifying (Luke 15:3–7).

∾ 144 ∾

By the Numbers

There were 70 elders that assisted Moses in governing ancient Israel, and there were 70 members of the ruling council in Jesus' day, the Sanhedrin. Jesus sent 70 disciples, in groups of two, to teach and heal in Judea. Since Jesus was not as well known there, this may have been a much tougher audience than those in Galilee who had seen his miracles. (See Luke 10:1–3.)

∾ 145 ∾

Very Large Crowds

After Jesus sent out the 70 disciples, Luke uses the word *myrias* to describe the crowds that flocked to hear Jesus in the last six months of his ministry. The word means "tens of thousands," and suggests the throngs that gathered were larger than even in Galilee, where Jesus spent most of his ministry.

∾ 146 ∾

A Reference to Ravens

When Jesus tells his disciples not to worry, because his Father takes care of and feeds even the birds, he refers specifically to ravens (Luke 12:24). Ravens were considered unclean, and his listeners would not have seen this example as poetic but as disgusting. It would be like saying that God loved vultures, not just song birds.

❧ 147 ❧

An Ordinary Messenger

When Mary and Joseph brought Jesus to Jerusalem for the purification ritual, they encountered a man named Simeon, who called Jesus, "A light to bring revelation to the Gentiles, and the glory of Your people Israel" (Luke 2:32). Simeon was neither priest nor religious leader; he is only described as "a man of Jerusalem" who was "just and devout."

❧ 148 ❧

Who Is My Enemy?

Not all Pharisees were hostile to Jesus. Some of them even warned him to leave Jerusalem because of the plot to kill him (Luke 13:31). Two Pharisees, Nicodemus and Joseph of Arimathea, took personal and political risks to care for his body after he was crucified.

❧ 149 ❧

Missing in the Manuscript

The first 11 verses of John 8 do not appear in the earliest and oldest New Testament manuscripts. These verses tell the story of the woman accused of adultery; when people want to stone her, Jesus says, "Let any one of you who is without sin be the first to throw a stone at her" (8:7, NIV). These verses may have been added later by someone with knowledge of the event, and the passage certainly seems consistent with the way Jesus taught and acted.

∽ **150** ∼

A True Story

The story of the rich man and a beggar named Lazarus (Luke 16:19–31) is the only story Jesus told in which he named one of the characters. This suggests that this story really happened, and was not just an illustration. Jesus did not name the rich man, but tradition says his name was Dives.

∽ **151** ∼

Believing Thomas

The disciple Thomas is often referred to as "doubting Thomas," since he insisted on seeing the wounds after Jesus was resurrected. But he was actually the first to understand that Jesus would die—and also volunteered to die with him. He said, "Let us also go, that we may die with Him" (John 11:16).

∽ **152** ∼

The Eye of a Needle

Jesus used the image of a camel going through the eye of a needle to explain how difficult it is for some to enter the kingdom of God (Matthew 19:24). Some say this refers to a gate in the city wall that was so small a camel could only get through it on its knees. But the Greek word used means a literal tailor's needle, and there is no literary evidence that the gate was referred to in this way.

❦ 153 ❧

A Series of Samaritans

Jesus told a story about the Good Samaritan, and the woman at the well in John 4 was also a Samaritan. And when Jesus healed ten lepers and only one returned to thank him, that one was also a Samaritan. "Where there not any found who returned to give glory to God except this foreigner?" Jesus asked. (See Luke 17:12–19.)

❦ 154 ❧

Jesus on Divorce

A certificate of divorce was not a legal document in the sense we understand it today. All a husband had to do was write or say "this is not my wife and I am not her husband." Jesus taught, however, that a man should not "put away his wife" as a matter of convenience, since divorce was not part of God's plan (Matthew 19:8–9, KJV).

❦ 155 ❧

Groaned in the Spirit

When Jesus saw how troubled Mary and Martha were when their brother Lazarus died, the Bible says he "groaned in the spirit." The literal translation of this phrase is "snorted like a horse," suggesting that death made Jesus feel angry and indignant.

∽ 156 ∾

Camel Confusion

The Aramaic word *gamla* can mean "camel," "rope," or "beam," depending on the context. It was translated into Greek and later into English, so it is possible Jesus said it is easier to thread a *rope* through the eye of a needle in his famous saying. (See Matthew 19:23–26.)

∽ 157 ∾

Return on Investment

A mina was an amount of money worth about one hundred days' wages. Jesus told a parable about a king who left this amount to ten servants when he was called away (Luke 19:11–27). The servant with the best return on the money he was given to invest produced ten minas—quite a sum!

∽ 158 ∾

A Kill List

By the time Jesus arrived in Bethany to stay with Mary and Martha the week before he died, the Sanhedrin had already issued orders for his arrest. John tells us that their brother Lazarus, whom Jesus raised from the dead, was added to the list of those to be eliminated (John 12:9–11).

◌ 159 ◌

Donkey or Colt?

What animal did Jesus ride into Jerusalem? The answer is a never-before-ridden donkey colt. Matthew suggests there were two animals, however, a mother and a colt (Matthew 21:2–7). The mother may have been brought along to help keep the colt calm.

◌ 160 ◌

The Cornerstone

The same word translated as "cornerstone" is also used to refer to a capstone, the key piece at the top of an arch. Jesus used this word to refer to himself (Luke 20:16–17), perhaps suggesting that he is the most important part of the door as well as the foundation.

◌ 161 ◌

A Loving Touch

One leper felt something he had probably not felt in a very long time when Jesus "put out His hand and touched him" (Matthew 8:3). Many people at that time believed leprosy was a result of one's sin, and so the psychological impact of the disease was often as bad as the disease itself. The first-century Jewish historian Josephus tells us that these "untouchables" could live for ten or more years with the disease, and were treated as dead men.

☙ 162 ❧

A Sad Song

In a funeral procession, male relatives carried the body on a bier, while the women walked ahead. Signs of mourning included wailing and tearing of clothes. Professional mourners and flute players were hired to show how much sorrow (or status) the family had. Jesus encountered such processions several times.

☙ 163 ❧

Who's on First?

At festival dinners, people reclined on a three-sided couch, called a triclinium, with their feet stretched out away from the table. At the Last Supper, the disciples argued about who would share the couch at the head of the table with Jesus (Luke 22:24).

☙ 164 ❧

Washing for Dinner

Banquet guests typically bathed before arriving, and only their feet needed to be washed before dinner. When Jesus washed his disciples' feet at the Last Supper, Peter asked Jesus to wash his hands and head as well, but Jesus said it wasn't necessary (John 13:10). Hand washing would also be part of the dinner experience.

⊂∞ 165 ∞⊃

A New Commandment

Jesus gave the disciples a "new commandment" and told them to "love one another" (John 13:34). This idea was not new, of course, and went back as far as the book of Leviticus. The word used here does not mean "recent" as much as it means "better." Jesus is suggesting new priorities.

⊂∞ 166 ∞⊃

Powerful, Personal Prayer

In John 17, Jesus prays for his disciples before he dies, a prayer sometimes referred to as the "High Priestly" prayer; it follows the pattern of the prayer offered by the high priest on the Day of Atonement. Others think of it as the Lord's Prayer, since it reflects Jesus' own heart, and think of the other, well-known prayer by that name as the "Model" prayer.

⊂∞ 167 ∞⊃

Abba, Father

Jesus used a very intimate form of the Aramaic word "father" when he prayed in the Garden of Gethsemane (Mark 14:35–36). It would be similar to our use of "Daddy." The Apostle Paul says that as adopted children all believers can think of God in this way (Romans 8:15).

⊃ **168** ⊂

A Dark Hour

When Judas came to betray Jesus, officials were expecting a fight. Judas was accompanied by a "detachment," at least 200 troops, in the middle of the night (John 18:3). "Have you come out, as against a robber, with swords and clubs?" Jesus asked (Luke 22:52).

⊃ **169** ⊂

Martha the Hostess

When Jesus and his followers visited the town of Bethany, they stayed with sisters Martha and Mary (Luke 10). Their brother Lazarus is not specifically mentioned, though he may have been there as well. Martha is described as welcoming Jesus in "her house," suggesting she was the owner and possibly the oldest of the three siblings. Her name actually means "lady" or "mistress."

⊃ **170** ⊂

The Start of Sabbath

Sabbath began each week when the first three stars appeared on Friday evening. A trumpet was blown, calling people from their work to supper. They did not eat again until after the service in the synagogue the next day. No household work could be done on the Sabbath, so meals were prepared ahead of time. Jesus was once criticized for snacking on grain on the Sabbath (Mark 2:23–27).

෩ 171 ෩

Why Do You Ask?

Annas interrogated Jesus, but by law the accused was not to be questioned by the judge. Everything was determined on the testimony of witnesses. Jesus was well within his legal rights to ask Annas, "Why do you ask me? Ask those who have heard Me what I said to them" (John 18:21).

෩ 172 ෩

What Happened to Pilate?

One early church historian, Eusebius, says that Pontius Pilate, the Roman governor who sentenced Jesus to death, committed suicide in Gaul several years later. Others say he and his wife became Christians. The Coptic Church recognizes Pilate as a saint and believes he was martyred for his faith.

෩ 173 ෩

A Green Tree

Several women at Jesus' Crucifixion were wailing in grief, but he urged them not to grieve him but their own children. "For if they do these things in the green wood, what will be done in the dry?" he said, citing a proverb (Luke 23:31). He was saying that if God pours out his wrath on his own Son, what will he do with those who rejected him?

∞ 174 ∞

Last Will and Testament

Even a crucified man had the right to make a verbal will, even from the cross. Jesus used the formula of Jewish family law to fulfill his obligation to his mother by transferring it to his friend John: "Woman, behold your son!" (John 19:26–27).

∞ 175 ∞

Cause of Death

The actual cause of death by crucifixion was asphyxiation. A block was provided for the victim's feet, however, allowing them to push their body up to catch a breath, thus prolonging the agony. Since the Passover was approaching, the soldiers came around to break each victim's legs so they would die more quickly, but Jesus was already dead (John 19:31–34).

∞ 176 ∞

No Funeral Allowed

An executed criminal could not be buried in his family's tomb until a year after his death, and no public mourning or funeral possession was allowed. Joseph of Arimathea and Nicodemus cared for the body of Jesus, and a few women went to the tomb, but no public rituals were conducted for him and he was not buried in a family tomb.

❧ 177 ❧

A Secret Disciple

Although Joseph of Arimathea and Nicodemus were members of the ruling council, the Sanhedrin, apparently neither of them were present at the trial of Jesus. It is supposed that they were not invited, because they were known Jesus sympathizers. Joseph is described as "a disciple of Jesus, but secretly" (John 19:38).

❧ 178 ❧

Burial Practices

The body of Jesus was wrapped in strips of linen mixed with spices—probably myrrh and aloes. While Egyptian burial was designed to preserve the body, Jewish burial practices were designed to inhibit odors during decay. When Jesus asked that the stone be removed from Lazarus' tomb, his sister Martha was concerned about the smell (John 11:39).

∞ 179 ∞

Going to the Temple

Jews observed five main religious feasts: Passover, the Feast of Weeks (Pentecost), the Feast of Tabernacles (harvest), the Feast of Trumpets (7th new moon of the year), and the Day of Atonement. As an observant Jew, Jesus would have observed all of these occasions. From the time he was a child, he probably went to Jerusalem three or four times a year for these events.

∞ 180 ∞

Party Time

The Jews loved feasts, which often went on for five or six hours, accompanied by music and dancing. Jesus often attended such events, and was even criticized by his enemies for attending such events with nonreligious Jews and even gentiles. (See Mark 2:13–17.)

∞ 181 ∞

A Common Pot

Stews were very common in Jesus' day, but spoons were rare. Diners would scoop food out of a common pot with bread. It was considered rude to dip in at the same time as someone else—something that happened with Jesus and Judas at the Last Supper (Mark 14:18–20).

∽ 182 ∾

Age of Marriage

Girls and boys in Jesus' day married at about the age of puberty, 12 for girls and 14 for boys. This was preceded by a binding one-year engagement, during which haggling between the families over the bride's dowry continued and the groom was expected to prepare a home for his wife.

∽ 183 ∾

A Binding Agreement

An agreement between families was celebrated and the groom began an engagement by saying, "This is my wife and I her husband, from today and forever." It was after this moment had happened that Joseph considered "putting away" (divorcing) his pregnant fiancée Mary, but an angel told him not to. (See Matthew 1:18–20.)

∽ 184 ∾

Home Sweet Home

Rich people had chairs and tables, but most people sat or slept on the ground, even in their homes. Most homes had chests for storing food and clothes. These chests doubled as tables. Homes like those in Capernaum (where Jesus stayed with his disciples) did have rooms, because they often housed two or more families.

⊱ 185 ⊰
A Synagogue Service

The synagogue had no priests and no sacrifices. After the recitation of prayers, scrolls were given to seven different readers who read assigned selections in Hebrew. When the reader finished, he sat down and gave a brief sermon in Aramaic, the language used in daily life. Anyone could do this—and Jesus did when he announced to his hometown that he was the Christ (Luke 4:16–21).

⊱ 186 ⊰
Ready or Not?

In one sermon Jesus told six stories in a row about being ready for his return (see Matthew 24—25). These stories emphasize being alert, faithful, and busy. Here we are specifically told to care for the poor and powerless.

⊱ 187 ⊰
Whitewashed Tombs

After a funeral, the tomb was often painted white to warn others that a body was decaying there. When it was fully decayed, the bones were collected and put in a stone box so the tomb could be used again. Jesus once referred to the Pharisees as "whitewashed tombs" (Matthew 23:27).

❧ 188 ❧

Not an Issue?

Jews considered work noble, and there was no disgrace in performing menial tasks, so most of the backbreaking and unpleasant jobs were done by free men. Slavery was not an issue for those Jesus taught or those who wrote about him, so we don't know if he addressed it directly.

❧ 189 ❧

How Much Meat Did Jesus Eat?

Jesus was not a vegetarian, but he probably did not eat much meat. Unless they were rich, most people only had meat at family feasts or religious festivals when a kid, calf, or lamb was killed. The very poor would eat fish or pigeons.

❧ 190 ❧

Annas and Caiaphas

Jesus was arrested and taken to Annas, the father-in-law of the high priest, Caiaphas. Annas had been the high priest until he was fired by the Romans in A.D. 15, but was still considered to be the power behind the throne. The Jews accepted this, since the high priest was supposed to be appointed for life.

⊂◦ 191 ◦⊃

Crown Him King

After hearing a sermon by Dean of Canterbury F. W. Farrar on the Lord's Second Coming, Queen Victoria told the pastor, "I should like to be living when Jesus comes, so that I could lay the crown of England at his feet."

⊂◦ 192 ◦⊃

Who Were the Zealots?

The Zealots were a splinter group of the Pharisees who wanted to drive out the Romans. The movement was centered in Galilee, where Jesus spent most of his ministry. This may explain why one of his disciples had been a Zealot. The Zealots began an uprising a few years after his death, which ended in A.D. 70 with the destruction of the temple.

⊂◦ 193 ◦⊃

Remember the Prophecy

Christians are not known to have been particularly active in the rebellion against Rome that began after Jesus died. It is thought that they remembered the prophecy Jesus made about the destruction of the temple (Matthew 24:1–2) and may have fled to non-Jewish cities on the other side of the Jordan River.

⊙ **194** ⊙
The Jewish Senate

At the beginning of their control of Israel, the Romans recognized the unique status of Jerusalem as the center of a religion with its own laws and customs. Jews were exempt from military service and allowed to govern themselves, within limits. Decisions of the Jewish senate, the Sanhedrin, applied to Jews all over the world, not just in Jerusalem or Palestine.

⊙ **195** ⊙
Cleaning House

A house was thoroughly cleaned on the day before Passover, and all the bread made with yeast (leavened) was eaten or burned. There had to be a fresh start. Jesus used this idea when warning his disciples about the "leaven" of the Pharisees (Matthew 16:6). His kingdom would require a completely new way of thinking.

❧ 196 ❧

A Jewish Revival

The name Galilee meant "the district of the pagans." But a Jewish king had reunited it with Judah about 150 years before Jesus came, bringing in Jewish families and giving them large tracts of land. By the time Jesus arrived, each town had its own synagogue and Judaism was flourishing.

❧ 197 ❧

Signs of a Trade

A Jewish boy was expected to learn and practice his father's trade. Each trade had its own symbol to wear, except on the Sabbath. A tailor had a needle in his tunic, and a carpenter, like Jesus and Joseph, wore a chip of wood behind his ear. The rabbis taught that a man who did not teach his son a trade brought him up to be a robber.

❧ 198 ❧

A Wedding Procession

On her wedding day, a bride waited with her friends at her home until her husband and his friends arrived and took her back to his parents' house. Celebrants danced and poured oil, wine, and perfume on the couple, scattering nuts and grain on the ground. Jesus used this image in the parable of the wise and foolish virgins (Matthew 25:1–13).

❧ 199 ❧

A Girl's Life

Mary was about 13 or 14 when she had Jesus. She would not have gone to school or been taught to read or write. Her days would have been spent mostly fetching water, tending the fire, or grinding grain. She was from a religious family, however, and therefore knew about Old Testament teachings regarding the Messiah.

❧ 200 ❧

The Jordan River

The name of the Jordan River, where Jesus was baptized, comes from a word that means "descender." The river itself drops over 2,000 feet from its source near Mt. Hebron to the Dead Sea, which is below sea level. Although the distance between these two points is a little less than 100 miles, the river winds and bends so much that its actual length is almost twice that.

❧ 201 ❧

Hate Your Mom?

The English word *hate* is sometimes used in the Bible to indicate priority or preference rather than the strong emotional feeling we think of today. This helps us understand what Jesus meant when he said that his followers must "hate" their parents and family (Luke 14:26).

∽ 202 ∽

A Splendid City

Although Jerusalem had been destroyed and rebuilt about five centuries before Christ, King Herod undertook a massive public works project. The improvements included the temple, a fortress, viaducts to bring water, public monuments, and an amphitheater, as well as palaces and citadels. Herod died when Jesus was still a young boy.

∽ 203 ∽

A Tale of Two Cities

Jerusalem was divided into two parts, in addition to the massive temple complex. There was a Lower City where craftsmen and merchants worked and sold their wares, as well as an Upper City where the wealthy families lived. In the Upper City, a Roman market sold jewelry, fine leather, and other luxury goods.

∽ 204 ∽

Temple Sections

Herod's temple, where Jesus often taught, was twice the size of the second temple, with an outer Court of the Gentiles that was about 1,000 feet wide by 1,500 feet long. Inside that perimeter was a courtyard where only Jews, including women, were allowed, and inside *that* was a courtyard for Jewish men only. Then, surrounding the sanctuary, was a courtyard for only priests.

∽ 205 ∽
Things Take Time

The temple itself was built in only 18 months, and priests were trained to do the work since laymen were not allowed to touch it. All the details of the outer courts took 80 years to complete, long after Herod himself had died. The temple complex was completed around A.D. 64, just a few years before the entire thing was razed by the Romans.

∽ 206 ∽
The Steps of the Rabbis

Jesus often taught in the Court of the Gentiles, and occasionally outside the temple on the "steps of the rabbis." These broad limestone steps, which led up to the temple from the south, have been excavated and are visible today. Classes were often held outside on these steps.

∽ 207 ∽
The Size of the City

At the time of Christ, the population of Jerusalem was 35,000 to 40,000 people. During the holy days, such as Passover, the population may have swelled to several times that size, with perhaps as many as a quarter of a million Jews coming for Passover. The walled part of the city was only about one square mile.

∞ **208** ∞

A Distant Country

The Decapolis was a league of ten Greek city-states mostly east of the Jordan River. They were brought under Roman control in 63 B.C., and given a great deal of autonomy. Jesus visited at least twice, and cast out demons that went into a herd of pigs and fed 4,000 with loaves and fishes. The "distant country" visited by the prodigal son was probably the Decapolis (Luke 15:13, NIV).

∞ **209** ∞

A Formidable Fortress

Antonia was a fortress that overlooked the temple, built by Herod the Great and named after Mark Antony. Although the temple area was governed by the priests, the fortress was an ever-present reminder of Roman power and authority. Jesus was tried and then scourged here before Pontius Pilate.

∞ **210** ∞

Who Were the Scribes?

The ruling class, the elders, was made up of mostly wealthy and powerful families, but by the time of Jesus a new elite was beginning to arise—the Scribes. The Scribes came from all walks of life to study under famous rabbis for 25 years before they were ordained at the age of 40. The Pharisees, on the other hand, were not known for their study as much as for following the teachings of the Scribes.

∞ 211 ∞

A Site to Behold

The Mount of Olives, where Jesus prayed before his crucifixion, was outside the walls of Jerusalem, near the eastern wall of the temple. It is hard to know exactly what the city looked like, but the first-century Jewish historian Josephus said that when you came over the top of the mountain, the temple looked like a snow-capped mountain—gleaming white buildings trimmed in gold.

∞ 212 ∞

Son of Man

Jesus referred to himself as the "Son of Man," a somewhat ambiguous term with several possible meanings at that time. It emphasized his humanity, but most Jews would have remembered that the prophet Daniel described the coming Messiah as "one like a Son of Man" (Daniel 7:13).

∞ 213 ∞

The Road to Jerusalem

When Jesus and his disciples walked from Galilee to Jerusalem for the holy days, like most pilgrims they usually did not take a direct route. They traveled east first, and then south along the Jordan River valley, avoiding the more mountainous Samaria, as well as the Samaritans themselves. The trek was about 90 miles and would have taken three or four days.

∽ 214 ∾
Living Water

Each morning during the seven-day Feast of Tabernacles, a procession of barefoot priests would go down to a spring in the Kidron Valley and return with a pitcher of water, chanting, "With joy you will draw water from the wells of salvation." On the last day of one year's festival, Jesus stood and cried, "If anyone thirsts, let him come to Me and drink" (John 7:37).

∽ 215 ∾
Expensive Perfume

Nard was a very expensive perfume imported from India. This was the perfume that Mary of Bethany poured on Jesus' feet and wiped off with her hair (John 12:1–8). Horace once offered to send Virgil a whole barrel of his best wine in exchange for a small amount of nard.

∽ 216 ∾
A Trumpet Sound

The shofar, or ram's horn, was used to signal the start of the Sabbath at sundown on Friday with three short blasts. Different combinations of notes were used to signal danger, the death of an elder or priest, the start of a new moon, the Passover, and other events. As a Jew, Jesus would have understood each signal.

❧ **217** ❧

An Angry Aristocrat

Pontius Pilate was a shrewd and hot-tempered Roman aristocrat who was governor of Judah from A.D. 26 to 36. His rule was marked by much civil unrest, and he was finally removed for excessive brutality in putting down occasional uprisings in the province. The Jews brought Jesus to trial before Pilate because they were not allowed to execute a prisoner without his permission.

❧ **218** ❧

A Smooth Start

The Roman Empire was fairly peaceful for the first 30 or so years after Jesus died. His followers were barely noticed as they established churches from Damascus to Rome by about A.D. 63, when widespread persecution began under Nero. There was some persecution by Jewish leaders, however, including one who would eventually become the Apostle Paul.

⨍ 219 ⨍
Similar Sermons

The earliest Christian sermons followed the same pattern: The prophecies spoke of Jesus, he was descended from King David, and he was raised from the dead to prove his power. While there were some variations, depending on the audience, they then included something about what Jesus offered or required from his followers.

⨍ 220 ⨍
The Kingdom of Jesus

Jews were reluctant to use the word God, for fear of taking his name in vain. That is why Matthew, writing to a mostly Jewish audience, uses the term "Kingdom of Heaven," while Mark and Luke use the term "Kingdom of God," which was easier for non-Jewish readers to understand. Neither expression occurs in the Old Testament.

⨍ 221 ⨍
A Series of Sermons

Matthew gathered the teachings of Jesus into five sections, the longest and best-known of which is the Sermon on the Mount (Matthew 5—7). The sections of teachings are alternated with narratives about what Jesus did and where he went.

∞ **222** ∞

Did Jesus Die on Friday?

By Jewish reckoning, any part of a day could be counted as a whole day, so Friday afternoon to Sunday morning is counted as three days. Jesus uses this time span to refer to the period Jonah spent in the great fish and that he himself would be in the grave (Matthew 12:40).

∞ **223** ∞

Many Miracles

Most of Jesus' miracles took place in a small area on the north side of the Sea of Galilee. This included Capernaum, Chorazin, and Bethsaida. The miracles provoked so little response that Jesus said several notably wicked cities in the Old Testament (including Sodom) would have repented if they had seen what he was doing (Matthew 11:20–24).

∞ **224** ∞

How Many Herods?

At least seven provincial rulers or governors in the New Testment were named or called Herod. All of them were sons or relatives of Herod the Great through his several wives. His son Herod Antipas is the one who executed John the Baptist.

∽ 225 ∾

What Is a Charger?

A charger was a large, flat plate for carrying a joint of meat. When asked for whatever she wanted, Salome asked Herod Antipas—her stepfather—for the head of John the Baptist "in a charger" (Matthew 14:6–11, KJV). The name comes from a word that means "to load."

∽ 226 ∾

According to the Scripture

When Jesus refers to the Scriptures, he is referring to the Old Testament. The Jewish Scriptures at that time had the same material as the Old Testament today but in a different order. It is thought that the prophet Ezra collected and restored these writings as the Jews returned from captivity in Babylon and rebuilt the temple.

∽ 227 ∾

A Greek Bible

The Old Testament was translated from Hebrew into Greek. This translation, called the Septuagint, was in common use in the time of Christ and is the version New Testament authors quote most often. The translation was completed in Alexandria, Egypt at Ptolemy's request around 250 B.C.

❧ 228 ❧
The Dispersion of the Jews

There were Jewish colonies in most major cities in the time of Christ. For example, it is estimated that there were more than a million Jews in Egypt alone. Many of these exiles traveled to Jerusalem at least once in their lives. Peter preached to such Jews at Pentecost in Acts 2, and the Apostle Paul often began his missionary work in these communities.

❧ 229 ❧
More about Matthew

The book of Matthew does not name its author, but John's pupil Papias says Matthew wrote it. The early church universally accepted this view. Matthew describes himself in the book only as a publican (tax collector). He wrote the book in Hebrew and issued a more complete version in Greek in about A.D. 60.

❧ 230 ❧
Family Matters

Joseph and Mary had at least seven children: Jesus, four named brothers, and two or more sisters (see Matthew 13:55–56). We know little about Joseph. He is generally assumed to have died before Jesus began his ministry at the age of 30, and certainly before the Crucifixion, since at that time Jesus committed the care of his mother to John.

◔ **231** ◔
How Many Magi?

The Scripture does not say how many magi, or wise men, there were. It can be safely assumed the group was fairly large, to travel safely some distance in the desert, and because their arrival in Jerusalem is said to have caused a great stir. Their particular office or title is not clear, but was of sufficient importance to give them immediate access to King Herod (Matthew 2:1–12).

◔ **232** ◔
Name That Angel

Angels are not always named in biblical accounts, but it was Gabriel who announced Christ's birth to Mary. He is assumed to be the angel who announced the birth of Christ to the shepherds and guarded the holy family on its flight to Egypt. The name Gabriel means "God is my strength."

◔ **233** ◔
Holy Ground

Jesus was baptized near Jericho in the lower Jordan. The site is also near Mt. Nebo, where Moses saw the Promised Land, and near Bethel, where Abraham built an altar. Nearby, Jacob saw a ladder ascending into heaven, and Elijah was taken up in a chariot and fed by ravens.

∞ **234** ∞

Mountaintop Experiences

Jesus fasted for 40 days to prepare for the Temptation in the mountains, Moses fasted for 40 days to prepare to receive the Ten Commandments on Mt. Sinai, and Elijah fasted for 40 days on his way to Mt. Horeb. These three appeared together on the Mount of Transfiguration.

∞ **235** ∞

About the Angels

Angels appear, act, or speak a dozen times in the Gospels, and Jesus makes a dozen specific references to them in his teachings. He says, for example, that they will gather the elect (Matthew 24:31), separate the wicked (Matthew 13:41, 49), guard children (Matthew 18:10), and rejoice when sinners repent (Luke 15:10).

∞ **236** ∞

A Short Story

Matthew covers the first year of Christ's ministry in Galilee in two verses, Matthew 4:11–12, although the events during this period were also covered by John (1:19—4:54) and Luke (4:16–30). Matthew devotes almost half of his book to the rest of the time Jesus spent in Galilee, however, while John hardly mentions this time.

⬿ 237 ⬾

The Ministry in Galilee

The ministry in Galilee lasted about two years, beginning "four months [before] the harvest," according to John 4:35 and 43. This would have been in December of A.D. 27. The Transfiguration occurred shortly before he left Galilee for the last time, probably in November or December of A.D. 29.

⬿ 238 ⬾

Time to Choose

Jesus took over a year to choose his disciples. While John, Andrew, Peter, Philip and Nathaniel began to follow him about the time of his baptism in late A.D. 26, he didn't call Simon, Andrew, James, and John to actually leave their fishing business until almost a year later, and he called Matthew after that. The formal call of the twelve was not until as late as May of A.D. 28.

⬿ 239 ⬾

How Many Parables?

Jesus told about 30 parables, although some lists include as many as 50. The variance has to do with how we define a parable, since what some people label a parable others see as a simple metaphor. Generally a parable is an extended metaphor meant to illustrate a particular point, and cannot be applied more broadly.

∞ **240** ∞

Politicians or Preachers?

The disciples most likely joined Jesus believing they would become leaders in some new political order. Even John the Baptist saw Jesus in this way (Matthew 11:3). In fact, the last question the disciples asked, even after the resurrection, was, "Lord, will You at this time restore the kingdom to Israel?" (Acts 1:6).

∞ **241** ∞

A Big Rock

When Peter says Jesus is "the Christ, the Son of the living God," Jesus replies by saying, "[Y]ou are Peter, and upon this rock I will build My church" (Matthew 16:16–18). There is a play on words here, as the Greek text says you are *Petros* and I will build my church on *petra*. *Petros* is a little rock, like a sling stone, but *petra* is a very big rock and can even apply to a mountain.

∽ **242** ∽

A Large Debt

A talent was worth about $1,000, but a shilling, or pence, was worth about 17 cents. Jesus told a story about a man who was forgiven a debt of $10,000,000 but was unwilling to forgive someone who owned him about $17. "And his master was angry, and delivered him to the torturers," Jesus said (Matthew 18:21–35).

∽ **243** ∽

The Perean Ministry

Jesus left Galilee about three months before his death in Jerusalem. He traveled to Perea, a small town near where was he was baptized about three years earlier; Bethany, where he raised Lazarus from the dead; and Jericho, where he called Zacchaeus down from a tree.

∽ **244** ∽

Profit Problem

The profit from the market booths in the temple area went to enrich the family of the high priest. Jesus drove out the moneychangers and merchants twice, at the very beginning of his ministry and again on the Monday before his death. "My house shall be called a house of prayer," he said, "but you have made it a den of thieves" (Matthew 21:13).

⊗ **245** ⊗

A Crazy Calendar

The Jewish calendar was based on lunar months and consisted of 354 days a year. Occasionally they would add a month, to catch up with the seasons. Farmers used the stars or other signs to determine when to plant, since the calendar was so unpredictable. Jesus referred to this when he said: "From the fig tree learn its lesson: as soon as its branch becomes tender and puts forth its leaves, you know that summer is near" (Matthew 24:32, NRSV)

⊗ **246** ⊗

Sacrificial Lambs

Jesus instituted the Lord's Supper for his disciples during a Passover meal. Christians believe that the Passover, when a sacrificial lamb was eaten, had been pointing forward toward Christ's own sacrifice for 14 centuries at the time he ate it with his disciples. The day Jesus died lambs were still being slain in the temple.

∽ **247** ∾

Cups of Blood

A layman could slaughter his family's Passover lamb at the temple, but the blood had to be caught by a priest. Rows of priests stood in line from the temple court to the altar. The priest who caught the blood handed the full cup to the priest next to him. Each priest in the line passed the cup until the final priest sprinkled its contents on the altar.

∽ **248** ∾

Poorly Kept Secret

The soldiers who guarded Jesus' tomb were bribed by the chief priests to say the disciples had stolen his body while the priests were sleeping. This inside knowledge of what happened may be why, in just a short time, "a great many of the priests were obedient to the faith" (Acts 6:7).

∽ **249** ∾

The Nazareth Decree

About ten years after the Resurrection, the Roman emperor Claudius issued a law making it a capital crime to disturb a burial place. A copy of the law, carved in marble, was found in Nazareth. It is thought the law was in response to the official Jewish explanation of the Resurrection.

∽ 250 ∾
The Gospel of Peter

Papias, an early church historian, says Mark spent time with Peter when he was in Rome and wrote this Gospel around the same time Peter wrote his first letter to the churches. The Gospel is written largely from Peter's point of view, as Mark himself was not an eyewitness to the events.

∽ 251 ∾
Stand or Sit?

In Luke's account of the Sermon on the Mount, Jesus "came down with them and stood on a level place" (Luke 6:17). In Matthew's account, he "went up on the mountain and sat down there" (Matthew 15:29). It is possible he did both things in the same sermon, but more likely he gave the same sermon more than once. He was teaching continually and may have discussed the same ideas hundreds of times.

∽ 252 ∾
Where Was He Buried?

Two different sites are purported to be Jesus' burial place. The first is the Church of the Holy Sepulcher, dating from A.D. 326 under Constantine. An alternative site called the Garden Tomb is recognized by some Protestant groups and was discovered in 1984 near a skull-shaped rock outside Jerusalem.

❧ 253 ❧
The Great Physician

There are 35 recorded miracles, 17 of which include healing. But seven specific passages refer to Christ healing many more people than this. For example, multitudes came to him and he "healed *them* all" (Luke 6:17–19).

❧ 254 ❧
No Room in the House

The "inn" in Luke 2 is translated from a word that could refer to a guest room adjoining a private home, in this case perhaps some relative of Joseph or Mary. Because the room was already occupied, the pair had to lodge in the stable. This would explain the "house" they were living in when visited by the magi (Matthew 2:11).

❧ 255 ❧
A Site to See

The Church of the Nativity in Bethlehem was built by Helena, the mother of Constantine, around A.D. 330. There is a cave-like room beneath the church that is said to be the manger where Jesus was born. Jerome spent 30 years in this room translating the Bible into Latin.

❧ **256** ❧

A Benefactor

Mary of Magdalene was prominent among the women who followed Jesus. He had cast demons out of her (Luke 8:1–3), and she is mentioned more than any of the other women, including Mary, the mother of Jesus. She was a woman of some means who provided financial support for his ministry and was the first to whom Jesus appeared after his resurrection.

❧ **257** ❧

Not Poor Peasants

The disciples were not all poor peasants. Peter, James, John, and Andrew were partners in a successful fishing business. They owned homes and had servants. Fish from the Sea of Galilee was preserved and sold as far away as Spain. Matthew, the tax collector, also had a large home.

❧ **258** ❧

What's in a Name?

Peter was a successful fisherman, with a home in Capernaum and a wife who traveled with him in his work as an apostle. He was energetic, enthusiastic, and impulsive. Peter's given name was Simon, but Jesus changed his name to Peter when they met while John was baptizing in the Jordan River.

∽ 259 ∾
The Deaths of Martyrs

Tradition says that most of the apostles died as martyrs. The first to die was James, beheaded by Herod Agrippa in A.D. 44 in Jerusalem. This is the only account of a disciple's death actually recorded in Scripture (Acts 12:1–2). Others are believed to have preached as far away as Ethiopia and India before eventually being killed.

∽ 260 ∾
Well Connected

The Apostle John, son of Zebedee and Salome, was well connected. Besides their fishing business in Galilee, his family owned a home in Jerusalem (John 19:27) and were friends with the high priest (John 18:15–16).

∽ 261 ∾
Firsthand Accounts

Luke wrote his Gospel and the book of Acts to a Roman official named Theophilus. Much of Acts was written from Luke's own experiences as he traveled with Paul, and the Gospel he wrote while living near Jerusalem benefited from many firsthand accounts, including those of Jesus' mother Mary and half-brother James.

262
The Disciple Jesus Loved

The Apostle John may have been a childhood friend of Jesus, since their mothers appear to be related. He followed Jesus from the beginning of his ministry, and calls himself "the disciple whom Jesus loved." After writing five New Testament books, he was exiled to an island for several years and died of natural causes in Ephesus around A.D. 100.

263
The Power of Love

While in exile Napoleon is reported to have said: "Alexander, Caesar, Charlemagne, and I myself have founded great empires; but upon what did these creations of our genius depend? Upon force. Jesus alone founded His empire upon love, and to this very day millions will die for Him."

264
Recycled Information

Much of what we know about daily life in biblical times comes from scrap paper: receipts for purchases and fees, rents, tax records, and other documents that were discarded and unintentionally preserved on discarded pieces of papyrus. The parable of the Unjust Seward (Luke 16:1–13) is grounded in archeological finds that document widespread corruption and fraud.

∽ 265 ∾
About That Scar

The census forms Joseph would have completed when he traveled to Bethlehem with Mary are well documented. They were sworn statement that included names, ages, and physical descriptions, including any distinguishing features such as scars. Birth certificates required the same information.

∽ 266 ∾
A Gracious Dad

Legal documents and personal letters from the first century suggest the father who waits for and welcomes the prodigal son would have been an anomaly (Luke 15:11–32). The father Jesus described was extremely gracious, since families typically cut off and ostracized any wayward children without financial recourse.

∽ 267 ∾
Doctor Luke

Luke was a companion of the Apostle Paul and may have studied medicine in Tarsus at the same time Paul studied philosophy and law. There are similarities in their language and themes, and both authors were influenced by Greek styles of writing.

❦ **268** ❦

Real Christians

As early as A.D. 110, Pliny, the Roman governor of Bithynia, explained to the Emperor Trajan in writing how purported Christians who cursed Christ and offered sacrifices to the Emperor could be separated from "those who are real Christians." Jesus told a parable about wheat and tares in which what is real is separated from what is false (Matthew 13:24–30).

❦ **269** ❦

No Bridges

An ancient mosque in India has a saying attributed to Jesus: "The world is merely a bridge, you are to pass over it and not to build your dwellings on it." Jesus likely never saw or crossed a bridge in his lifetime, as there were no bridges in Palestine. Thomas and Bartholomew are said to have preached in India and may be the source of this quote.

❦ **270** ❦

A Pagan Provocation

Pilate's predecessor issued common copper coins adorned with palm branches, but Pilate's coins had a *lituus,* or pagan priest's staff. It was a deliberate provocation designed to annoy the Jews. Coins then were a means of instruction and propaganda, more like a postage stamp today.

❧ **271** ❧

Two Temples

Herod the Great spent 12 years in Caesarea building a Roman port. He built a temple to Caesar there and a temple to Jehovah in Jerusalem, demonstrating political ambition and acumen by balancing his allegiance to Rome with the political realities of ruling the Jews. These tensions persisted throughout the life of Christ.

❧ **272** ❧

Pilate's Pavement

The pavement where Pilate passed judgment on Jesus can still be seen today. There are patterns carved in the stone where soldiers played games and a section of stone scored to give horses a foothold. This area in the ruins of the Antonia Fortress is considered authentic. Street level has risen 15 to 20 feet in the centuries since.

❧ **273** ❧

Christians in China

Early Christian missionaries traveled at least as far as China. A monument dating to A.D. 781 contains a statement of Christian belief and notes the arrival of a missionary from Syria named Olapan in A.D. 736. He was a follower of a fifth-century Syrian bishop named Nestorius.

❧ 274 ❧

Paul in Prison

For Romans, a punishment meant a beating, execution, or even exile, while prison was simply a place to wait for a trial. This is why Paul still had his own house in Rome where guests were welcome. Roman citizens were usually only chained when being moved from place to place.

❧ 275 ❧

Nail-Scarred Hands?

The Greek word for hand includes the wrist but the Latin word does not. Medieval artists depicted Jesus with wounds in his hands, but Romans nailed victims to a cross using the wrist because hands could not support the body's weight. When the artists read their Bibles in Latin they could not visualize this fact.

❧ 276 ❧

Different Math

The Jews and Romans did not have or use zero in their calculations and began adding with one. This explains how Jesus was dead "three days," when it was only a day and a half from Friday afternoon to Sunday morning. Jesus used this logic in another context when he said: "I will keep on driving out demons and healing people today and tomorrow, and on the third day I will reach my goal" (Luke 13:32 NIV).

∽ **277** ∾

An Invitation to Dinner

Wealthy men often invited friends, clients, and social climbers to dinner with written invitations delivered and read by servants. Other guests were invited on impulse during the day. They invited people who could do them favors or who were celebrities, which explains why Jesus was often invited to lavish dinners.

∽ **278** ∾

Dinner in Daylight

Daily life in the city began at sunrise, and most official business was concluded before noon. Life was structured to slow down in the heat of the day, and dinner started as early as 3:30, as it was not safe to be out after dark. Most of the dinners Jesus attended were in daylight.

∽ **279** ∾

The Master's Feet

At one dinner party Jesus is described as sitting at the table while a woman standing behind him washed his feet (Luke 7:36–50). This sounds awkward, but Jesus would have been reclining with his feet away from the table. The woman could have slipped into the dinner unnoticed because servants often stood by their masters' feet during a meal.

∽ 280 ∽
Small House

Ordinary people lived in small, one– or two-room houses. The roofs were flat (because it seldom rained) and used as patios for people to get fresh air without standing in the street. Jesus said you could put a lamp on a stand and "it gives light to all *who are* in the house" (Matthew 5:15), a reference to these small homes.

∽ 281 ∽
Former Forests

Israel today includes large sections of rocky barrens, but in the time of Christ it was mostly wooded. Many native plants are gone and replaced by imported plants like the eucalyptus tree, which Jesus and his followers would not have known. Oaks and terebinths are now found alone or in small clusters but in biblical times would have filled Galilee and Samaria.

◌ **282** ◌

The Lilies of the Field

The lilies of the field so often referred to in scripture and by Jesus himself were wildflowers and did not include the cultivated white lilies we often imagine. Tulips, crocuses, hyacinths, and other narcissus were common, but the flower he referred to was probably the red gladiolus or anemone that blanketed the area each spring.

◌ **283** ◌

Fine Wine

Palestine was not a great exporter of wine but produced enough for its own consumption. There were both cultivated and wild grapes, considered a symbol of fruitfulness and blessing. Jesus used the vine to represent himself and the wine to represent his blood.

◌ **284** ◌

Pass the Eggplant

Jesus never ate a tomato or corn, both products of American agriculture. The word "corn" in the New Testament refers to barley or wheat. Kitchen gardens included eggplant, peppers, cucumbers, and onions. Lentils formed the largest section of a garden since they are easily preserved.

285

Lord of the Flies

Palestine was teeming with mosquitos and flies, an annoyance so great that one of the names of the Devil was Beelzebub: "Lord of the flies." This was a reference to the fourth plague in Egypt but also to the large number of insects and arachnids Jesus would have known, including butterflies, beetles, locusts, wasps, and scorpions.

286

What's in a Name?

The Romans referred to the people as Jews, a reference to the tribe of Judah that comprised most of the exiles who returned from Babylon. But the designations Israel and Hebrew are how they thought of themselves. Israel is the name God gave Jacob. Hebrew is from a word that means "he who crosses over" and refers to Abraham's wanderings after he left Ur.

∽ **287** ∾

Pax Romana

The Romans were originally welcomed into Palestine as peacemakers after a civil war between two descendants of Alexander the Great. They got off to a bad start when Pompey entered the Holy of Holies expecting to find an astonishing idol—a sacrilege that Jesus heard about many times as a boy.

∽ **288** ∾

A Massive Wall

The wall around Jerusalem was so massive it took 15,000 of Titus' Roman soldiers a hundred days to breech it. The smallest blocks each weighed one ton, and there were towers about every 100 yards. There were several gates. Jesus compared himself to the Sheep Gate (John 10:7), through which animal sacrifices came into the city.

∽ **289** ∾

Here Comes the Judge

Judges were powerful men given their responsibilities as an honor. They were not paid but were respected and even feared. Any Israelite could be a civil judge, but only a priest could decide a criminal case. Their power was so great that Jesus advised making peace with your opponent before you even got to court, "lest your adversary deliver you to the judge" (Matthew 5:25).

∽ **290** ∾
Names Needed

Only one day of the week had a name, the Sabbath. The day before the Sabbath was sometimes called the Day of Preparation, but days were usually numbered. Matthew, for example, says the resurrection occurred on the "first day of the week" (Matthew 28:1).

∽ **291** ∾
It's Nine Sixty-Five

An hour was a division of a day rather than a set period of time. On the winter solstice, for example, an hour of daylight might have been 45 minutes while an hour that night would have been 75 minutes. When Jesus said his disciples could not "watch with Me one hour" (Matthew 26:40) at Gethsemane, he was not describing our sixty-minute measure.

∽ **292** ∾
Not Too Long

A cubit is the distance from an elbow to the end of the second finger, but there was both a weak cubit (17.7 inches) and a strong cubit (21.25 inches). Architects used the strong cubit while people used the weak cubit in daily life, suggesting that the Jewish people were shorter than the Romans at the time.

❄ **293** ❄

Buying Barley

The word translated as "bushel" refers to a measure of around three gallons of grain. In any household there was a container of this size to measure the wheat or barley needed for making bread. Poorer households also used this container as a table. "No one after lighting a lamp puts it under the bushel basket," Jesus said (Matthew 5:15, NRSV).

❄ **294** ❄

Let's Have Lunch

In Hebrew, "to eat bread" meant "to have a meal." Bread was so respected that you were not allowed to put a piece of raw meat or a pitcher of water on it, or a hot plate against it. You could not throw away the crumbs if they were as large as an olive. Jesus said he was the bread we really needed.

❄ **295** ❄

A Fish Sandwich

Bread and fish was the most affordable meal for common people. The disciples find loaves and fishes when feeding the 5,000, and Jesus says, "If a son asks for bread from any father among you, will he give him a stone? Or if he asks for a fish, will he give him a serpent instead of a fish?" (Luke 11:11).

ᕥ **296** ᕦ
The Upper Room

People often put tents on their roofs for the Feast of Tabernacles, when they lived for a week in temporary shelters to remind themselves of their time in the wilderness. Wealthier families started to build more permanent structures on their roofs, which eventually became second stories. Jesus held the last supper in one of these upstairs chambers.

ᕥ **297** ᕦ
A Real Fear

Rich people's homes were stone, but everyone else's homes were made of handmade bricks of clay and straw. These were burgled easily and often, and Jesus referred to this when he said to lay up treasure in heaven where "thieves do not break in and steal" (Matthew 6:20).

ᕥ **298** ᕦ
A Place to Stay

Jesus spent so much time in Capernaum that it was considered his hometown (Matthew 9:1). There were about 1,500 people at that time, including a Roman garrison under the control of Herod Antipas. The commanding centurion was friendly and supportive of his Jewish neighbors and built the synagogue for them. Jesus healed the centurion's servant (Luke 7: 1–9).

⤚ **299** ⤙

Repetitive Rhythms

Most learning during Jesus' time was through rote memorization, and this affected the cadence and rhythm of everyday speech. Repetition and rhyme made such memorization possible. The Beatitudes and the Magnificat are two well-known examples.

⤚ **300** ⤙

Buy a Vowel

The twenty-two letters of the Hebrew alphabet are all consonants. To accommodate this, four consonants served double duty as vowel sounds, much as we sometimes use the letter y as a vowel sound. Jesus referred to the smallest of these letters, the Jod, in Matthew 5:18.

⤚ **301** ⤙

Where Did It Happen?

It is almost impossible to ascertain the exact location of some key events in Jesus' life. Roman expelled the Christians and Jews who would have known or cared about these places shortly after Jesus died. Christianity was not recognized by the state until 300 years later under Constantine. Many places have also changed because of earthquakes, climate, and war.

❧ 302 ❧
The Branch of Isaiah

Matthew said Jesus would be called a Nazarene, fulfilling Old Testament prophecy (Matthew 2:23). This does not refer to his childhood in Nazareth, however. The Greek word translated this way likely refers to the Hebrew word *netzer*, meaning branch. Isaiah 11:1 says "There shall come forth a Rod from the stem of Jesse, and a Branch *[netzer]* shall grow out of his roots."

❧ 303 ❧
Small-Town Boy

Excavations indicate the hamlet of Nazareth, attached to the larger village of Japhia, did not number more than 150 at the time of Christ. Japhia was a fortified city that played an important role in the war against the Romans in A.D. 66–70.

❧ 304 ❧
Who Were the Essenes?

Jesus was familiar with the Essenes, a group of priests who withdrew from temple worship in the second century B.C. and rejected the high priests in Jerusalem as pagans. The Essenes did not offer sacrifices but purified themselves in ritual baths. It is thought that Jesus' cousin John the Baptist lived with this group for several years.

❦ 305 ❦
Three Schools of Thought

There were three schools of thought regarding the Torah: the Sadducees, the Essenes, and the Pharisees. Each group recognized the Torah as supreme law but had its own interpretations, and each was a recognized and accepted way of Jewish life in the time of Christ. The only school that survived, that of the Pharisees, provided the foundation of modern rabbinical Judaism.

❦ 306 ❦
Something Fishy

Fishing was an important and respected occupation near the Sea of Galilee, as evidenced by the names of towns where Jesus lived and ministered: Bethsaida means "the fishery" and Magdala means "fish tower."

❦ 307 ❦
A Travelogue

Much of what we know of Capernaum comes to us from the journal of Egeria, a pious woman from Spain who visited the area between A.D. 383 and 395. She describes Peter's house, the synagogue, and the location of events like the Sermon on the Mount and the miraculous feeding of the 5,000.

⌇ **308** ⌇

A Cult of Idols

Mark describes when Jesus drove out demons from a man in the Gadarenes into a herd of pigs. In fact, he recorded several stories about Jesus casting out demons. Like other contemporary Jews, Mark believed that the pagans' idol worship was a façade for the demonic and wanted to draw their attention to these stories.

⌇ **309** ⌇

Pagan and Rich

The early church historian Eusbius (A.D. 265–340) describes a home in Caesarea Philippi with a statue of a woman on her knees, reaching out to a young man. He said this was the home of the woman who was healed by touching Jesus' coat. The home and statue indicate not only was she ceremonially unclean from issue of blood, but she was also probably pagan and rich.

◈ **310** ◈

How Many Baskets?

After the feeding of the 5,000, who were mostly Jews, the leftovers filled 12 baskets, corresponding with the 12 tribes of Israel. After feeding the 4,000 in the more Gentile region east of the Jordan, they took up seven baskets, in reference to the seven heathen peoples (Deuteronomy 7:1; Acts 13:19).

◈ **311** ◈

The Sign of Jonah

After Jesus fed the multitudes, the Pharisees and Sadducees asked him for a "sign from heaven." Jesus said that the only sign the people would receive was the "sign of the prophet Jonah" (Matthew 16:4). The sign of Jonah is the conversion of Nineveh, a pagan city. His ministry and several specific miracles reflected this openness to non-Jewish peoples.

◈ **312** ◈

Healed in Stages

Mark speaks of only one person whom Jesus healed by increments, a blind man from Bethsaida (Mark 8:22–25). Jesus appeared to be illustrating the principle that belief is not a sudden recognition, but a process by which one comes to a deeper understanding. He had just asked his disciples in verse 18, "Having eyes, do you not see?"

☙ 313 ❧

Don't Tell Anyone

Jesus said several times not to tell anyone about him or about his miracles (Mark 8:30). He did not want anyone to misunderstand him or force his hand, because a group of militants called Zealots wanted the Messiah to set up a political kingdom in northern Galilee.

☙ 314 ❧

Hot Topic

Before he died, Jesus spent time "beyond the Jordan" where the influence of the Essenes was the strongest. Here he was asked about divorce because it was controversial: The Pharisees taught that divorce was permissible, but the Essenes did not. He sided with the Essenes on this issue (Mark 10:1–9).

☙ 315 ❧

Unusual Greeting

At the time there were different greetings between strangers, between men, between women, and between married people or adults and children. We are told Mary was confused when the angel appeared and said, "Rejoice, highly favored *one*, the Lord *is* with you." She "considered what manner of greeting this was" because no one she knew had ever used such a greeting (Luke 1:26–29).

☙ 316 ❧

The Well of Mary

Nazareth has only one spring, and it never runs dry. The water flows into a well where women still gather and fill jugs that they balance on their heads, much like Mary would have done. The well is next to the Greek Orthodox Church of St. Gabriel.

☙ 317 ❧

A Lasting Peace?

Jesus lived during the reign of the Roman Emperor Caesar Augustus, who was generally thought to have brought peace to the world. His name means "worthy of reverence." Augustus said he hoped the foundation he laid would survive forever. Jesus said his own kingdom was not of this world.

☙ 318 ❧

Born on Main Street

When Jesus was born, Bethlehem was not the sleepy little village we often imagine. It was on a well-known trade route and only three miles from one of Herod's palaces. Travelers had to go through Bethlehem en route to the palace, which was the center of administration for places south of Jerusalem.

✆ 319 ✆
Good News, Great Joy

The angel's announcement to the shepherds in the field follows a tradition of the Bedouins, a nomadic group which still lives in Palestine. Bedouin women attending a birth told the father, "We bring you good news of a great joy, for to you is born this day...."

✆ 320 ✆
What's in a Name?

A baby boy received his name after he was circumcised, and a firstborn son generally received the name of his grandfather. People were surprised when the mother of John the Baptist insisted his name was John. "There is no one among your relatives who is called by this name," they said (Luke 1:61). The name means "God is gracious."

✆ 321 ✆
A Devout Woman

Anna praised God when Mary and Joseph brought the baby Jesus to the Temple. She is called a prophetess. Likely this did not refer to a profession but was a title of respect for a dignified and devout older woman.

∽ 322 ∽
The Center of the World

Many observant Jews went to the temple several times a day to stand for hours in silence or offer prayers, and the priests came out multiple times a day to offer blessings on the people. According to Josephus, they believed the temple was the center of the world. The most serious allegation against Jesus at his trial was that he likened himself to this splendid building.

∽ 323 ∽
That's a Fact

The gospels are firmly rooted in historical fact. Luke, for example, names the specific year, emperor, governor, tetrarchs, and high priests in office when John the Baptist began to preach near the Jordan River (Luke 3:1–2).

∽ 324 ∽
A Significant Stream

The Jordan River, where Jesus was baptized, had little economic or political significance. It was too small for transporting goods and easily forded during the dry summer months. Its significance is mostly historical and spiritual (Deuteronomy 9:11, 13).

∞ **325** ∞

Keeping Watch

Passover is also called *Leil Shimurim*, night of the watchers. This refers to Exodus 12:42, where it is translated as the night the Lord "kept vigil." This was the same night Jesus prayed in the Garden of Gethsemane, asking his disciples to keep watch. "Could you not watch one hour?" he asked Peter (Mark 14:37–38).

∞ **326** ∞

Safety in Numbers

Few people traveled alone. Jesus tells the story of a Samaritan who cares for a man attacked by bandits, even though he was on the much-traveled road between Jericho and Jerusalem. Jesus and his disciples prudently traveled in a group.

∞ **327** ∞

A Style of Speaking

Mashalim, the Hebrew word sometimes translated as parable, refers to a broader range of literary devices, including stories, riddles, jokes, maxims, and proverbs. Hebrew orators made much more use of these than did Greeks, who depended more on logic and argument. The teachings of Jesus depended heavily on this Hebrew tradition.

❧ 328 ❧
Name That Tune

Hebrews excelled in music, probably because other arts were forbidden to them by the commandment not to make any images. The music itself was not written down, but choral traditions persisted. Jesus and his disciples sang together (Matthew 26:30) as did the early church (Colossians 3:16).

❧ 329 ❧
Sponges and Soap

Jews were diligent about personal cleanliness, and some rabbis even forbade living in a town with no baths. Jesus probably washed daily with ashes of soda-yielding plants mixed with some kind of fat. People used sponges and brushes but not toothbrushes. Instead, they used spices to sweeten their breath.

❧ 330 ❧
Alms for the Poor

One of the most common practices in the life of a Jew was giving money or bread to the poor. Beggars were everywhere, and even came from other countries because of the Jews' reputation for generous charity. There are several references to beggars in the New Testament, including the one where Jesus referred to himself in this role (Matthew 25:35–40).

∽ 331 ∾

Stadium Sports

People in Jerusalem practiced Greek wrestling and chariot racing, although devout Jews avoided these sports. Jesus never referred to them as far as we know, and they are not mentioned in the Gospels. The Apostle Paul refers to races in the stadium, but he was writing to converted Greeks living in a pagan city (1 Corinthians 9:24).

∽ 332 ∾

Call the Doctor

Jews believed the body and soul were closely related. Sections of the Talmud read like medical manuals. People were treated with a variety of herbal and animal ointments and potions and even minor operations like Caesarean deliveries and amputations. Doctors practiced medicine, but priests also had medical responsibilities. Jesus was probably best known at the time for his healing power.

⊘ **333** ⊘

The Guardian of Mothers

In describing the Slaughter of the Innocents by Herod, Matthew refers to "Rachel weeping *for* her children" (Matthew 2:18). Jacob's wife Rachel was buried near Bethlehem and venerated as the guardian of all mothers.

⊘ **334** ⊘

A Simple Synagogue

Synagogues like the one in Capernaum where Jesus taught were simply designed and decorated. There was no altar, since it was a place for teaching, not worshiping. The scriptures were kept in a chest called an ark. Services were held at least three times a week. The reading cycled through the first five books of the Bible (the Pentateuch) in just under three years.

⊘ **335** ⊘

A Church on Each Corner

There were four or five hundred synagogues in Jerusalem when Jesus was alive, some of them standing in rows. Any Jew could erect a synagogue and did so around communities that represented nationalities, guilds, families and other social groups. The Apostles made extensive use of this network as they shared the gospel in the early church.

∽ 336 ∾

A Lot of Vows

Many Jews made vows to God as a way to obtain favor or give thanks. Jesus refers to one of these, *corban,* a vow in which something was promised to the temple. This vow was sometimes used, he pointed out, to forfeit obligations to one's parents (Mark 7:11). Many other vows were practiced and regulated by the teachers of the Law.

∽ 337 ∾

A Common Name

Jesus is a very old Jewish name that means "God saves us." It is the same as the name Joshua, the famous judge and general who led the people into Palestine. There were four high priests by this name between 37 B.C. and A.D. 70. It is also the name used by the author of Ecclesiasticus, one of the Apocryphal books.

∽ 338 ∾

Turn the Other Cheek

Jesus often expanded on Old Testament teaching. He said, for example, "But whoever slaps you on your right cheek, turn the other to him also" (Matthew 5:39). This idea is also found in Lamentations 3:30, advising, "Let him give *his* cheek to the one who strikes him."

∾ **339** ∾

How Many Messiahs?

There were many self-styled messiahs in Palestine, including six between Jesus' birth and the destruction of the Temple in A.D. 70. Jesus did most of his teaching and healing in Galilee and was likely little known outside his region.

∾ **340** ∾

The Son of God

On two occasions a voice from heaven described Jesus as "my beloved son": at the beginning of his ministry when he was baptized and near the end of his ministry on the Mount of Transfiguration. He never referred to himself as the Son of God, but he often spoke of God as his Father.

∾ **341** ∾

The Jesus Manifesto

Luke 4:16–21 is sometimes called the Jesus Manifesto. This is where Jesus read from Isaiah in the synagogue at Nazareth and said the prophecy was fulfilled that day. The components of this manifesto were preaching the good news, freeing captives, and giving sight to the blind. He also proclaimed the "year of the Lord," a reference to the year of Jubilee when all debts were forgiven.

∞ **342** ∞
Part of the Plan

Jesus knew he was going to die in Jerusalem, and mentioned it at least three times (Mark 8:31; 9:31; 10:33–34; and parallel passages in other Gospels). He went to Jerusalem to "give His life a ransom for many" (Matthew 20:28).

∞ **343** ∞
A Madman or the Messiah

C.S. Lewis said: "A man who was merely a man and said the sort of things Jesus said would not be a great moral teacher. He would either be a lunatic—on the level with the man who says he is a poached egg—or else he would be the Devil of Hell. You must make your choice. Either this man was, and is, the Son of God, or else a madman or something worse."

∞ **344** ∞
You Have to Ask

Jesus only healed people who asked for his help. For example, he specifically asked blind Bartimaeus what he wanted Jesus to do (Mark 10:46–52). He also frequently commended the faith of those who asked, such as the hemorrhaging woman: "Be of good cheer, daughter; your faith has made you well" (Matthew 9:22).

∽ **345** ∽

Son of the Holy One

Humans did not always obey Jesus—he told them not to discuss what he had done but they did anyway (Mark 1:43–45). But the demons always obeyed him, frequently acknowledged they knew who he was, and were in awe of him (Mark 1:24).

∽ **346** ∽

Recruiting Students

Students usually chose which rabbi they wanted to follow and learn from, but Jesus chose his disciples. Sometimes he taught only them, and sometimes he elaborated to them after teaching others. It was common for a rabbi to be followed by a group of disciples.

∽ **347** ∽

The Shekinah Glory

The angel that announced the birth of Christ to the shepherds was accompanied by "the glory of the Lord," appearing as a great light. Glory as light was known as *Shekinah,* indicating the presence of God. (See Numbers 14:21 and Exodus 33:18–22.)

❧ **348** ❧
Birth of a King

The star that led the magi to Jesus is most often thought to have been a conjunction of planets, but the Roman poet Virgil writes of a comet as a "star leading a meteor." Tacitus, a first-century Roman historian, says both events were associated with the change of an emperor or the birth of a king.

❧ **349** ❧
Work to Do

Joseph fled to Egypt with Mary and Jesus to avoid the Slaughter of the Innocents but returned with his family to Nazareth after Herod died. Herod's son, Herod Antipas, ruled Galilee at that time and rebuilt the city of Sepphoris. As a carpenter, Joseph would have easily found work there and provided for his family.

❧ **350** ❧
Wrong Priorities

The Roman historian Josephus has more to say about John the Baptist than about Jesus. John was so famous, in fact, that the word Baptist was coined to describe him—it did not exist as a noun before that. It was John, however, who said that, "[Jesus] *must* increase, but I must decrease" (John 3:30).

∽ **351** ∽

Jesus the Baptist

Early Christians were baptized for several reasons, some of them theological, as the Apostle Paul would explain in his letter to the Romans. They were baptized because Jesus had been baptized and had baptized others early in his ministry (John 3:22). It was also part of his last command in Matthew 28:19.

∽ **352** ∽

Fishermen Foretold

In Jeremiah 16:16–21 the Lord says, "I will send for many fishermen" and they will fish for evildoers, so "I will cause them to know My hand and My might; And they shall know that My name *is* the Lord." Jesus chose at least four fishermen among his disciples.

∽ **353** ∽

Scattered Sheep

Before Jesus is crucified, he knows his disciples will desert him and quotes Zechariah 13:7: "Strike the Shepherd, and the sheep will be scattered." These same disciples gathered in Jerusalem after the resurrection and started the first church. Then they scattered to preach to the rest of the known world.

⌘ **354** ⌘
The Anointing of a King

O ver a third of the Gospel of John describes the week between Palm Sunday and the Resurrection. It begins after Mary anointed Jesus with costly perfume (John 12). Many attended this dinner and would have related this to the practice of anointing ancient Jewish kings. The next day was Jesus' triumphal entry into Jerusalem on Palm Sunday.

⌘ **355** ⌘
Kiss My Hand

A lthough paintings often depict Judas kissing Jesus on the cheek, his greeting *Rabbi, Rabbi* suggests he more likely kissed him on the hand. This was the common greeting and acknowledgment between a disciple and his teacher.

⌘ **356** ⌘
The Story of Jesus

M ark was the first written Gospel (around A.D. 50), followed by several of Paul's letters to the churches. Luke completed his Gospel and the book of Acts before Paul died in A.D. 65. The other Gospels and letters from Peter and Jude followed. The last books written were John's three letters, his Gospel, and the Book of the Revelation, all after A.D. 90.

❧ 357 ❧

A Strong Start

The Acts of the Apostles, written by the same Luke as the Gospel, provides a bridge between the Gospels and Paul's letters to the growing group of believers after Jesus' death. After describing the beginning of the church in Jerusalem, Luke recounts Paul's three missionary journeys into what are now Turkey, Greece, and Italy.

❧ 358 ❧

I Am What You Need

Jesus is intentional about his use of the phrase "I am," a reference to the name God gave himself when speaking to Moses (Exodus 3:14). "Before Abraham was, I Am," Jesus said (John 8:58). He often uses this phrase in describing himself and says "I Am" the good shepherd, the door, the light, the bread, the way, the truth, the life, and the resurrection.

❧ 359 ❧

A Carriage Ride?

Although we picture Mary traveling by donkey, Luke never identifies her means of transportation. Since Joseph was an established tradesman, they could have traveled in a carriage. It was also possible to rent a carriage or wagon in one town and leave it in another.

∽ **360** ∾

The World Is Round

Mary and Joseph probably did not need a map to find Bethlehem because Joseph had family there, but there were maps available. Romans knew Earth was round and represented it as a globe on their coins.

∽ **361** ∾

Christian or Jew?

At first the Romans could not distinguish between the Jews and the Christians. The Emperor Claudius, for example, expelled the Jews from Rome in A.D. 49 because of a disturbance over someone named "Chrestus," a misspelling of Christus (Christ). This exile brought Priscilla and Aquila to Corinth, where they met the Apostle Paul (Acts 18:1–4).

∽ **362** ∾

The Caesar of Christ

Tiberius (emperor from A.D. 14 to 37) was on the coin handed to Jesus when he was asked about paying taxes to Rome. Tiberius was considered a distracted, stingy, and antisocial ruler who was deeply suspicious of those around him. He is alleged to have chosen his incompetent grandnephew Caligula to succeed him so his own reign would look better.

∽ **363** ∾
How Old Was He?

During Biblical times, people were much less precise about time. Most did not observe their birthdays or even know their own exact ages. Those who kept track used landmark events like floods or the reign of a king. Luke tells us Jesus was "about thirty" when he began his ministry (Luke 3:23).

∽ **364** ∾
The Year of Our Lord

Our modern calendar was conceived by a sixth-century monk named Dionysius Exiguus. He based his calculations on Luke's record that Jesus was 30 in the fifteenth year of Tiberius' reign. He used the term *anno Domini* ("year of the Lord"), hence the abbreviation A.D.

∽ **365** ∾
More about Jesus

John Bunyan, author of *Pilgrim's Progress*, said, "I love to hear my Lord spoken of, and where I have seen the print of His shoe in the earth, there have I coveted to put mine also."